# Creative Insubordination

*Creative Insubordination: 40 Successful Strategies*
Copyright © 2023 by Dr. John Telford

Published in the United States of America

| ISBN | Paperback: | 978-1-958030-72-1 |
| ISBN | Hardback: | 978-1-958030-89-9 |
| ISBN | eBook: | 978-1-958030-73-8 |

All rights reserved. No part of this publication may be reproduced, stored in a retrieval system or transmitted in any way by any means, electronic, mechanical, photocopy, recording or otherwise without the prior permission of the author except as provided by USA copyright law.

The opinions expressed by the author are not necessarily those of ReadersMagnet, LLC.

ReadersMagnet, LLC
10620 Treena Street, Suite 230 | San Diego, California, 92131 USA
1.619. 354. 2643 | www.readersmagnet.com

Book design copyright © 2023 by ReadersMagnet, LLC. All rights reserved.

Cover design by Ericka Obando
Interior design by Ched Celiz

# Creative Insubordination

## 40
Successful
Strategies for

Practicing C.I. while also
Avoiding Being Devoured by the Dragon

## Dr. John Telford
Creative Insubordinate Extraordinaire

ReadersMagnet, LLC

# Praise for Creative Insubordination and its Creatively Insubordinate creator

"John Telford is the champion of the underdog."
—**Dennis Archer**, Mayor of Detroit, 1994-2001

"In and around Detroit. Telford is a human-rights legend."
—**Professor Joshua Bassett**, Wayne County (Michigan) Community College

"A fast-moving, mind-expanding book that will change your life."
—**Tom Bleakley**, nationally prominent attorney

"Poignantly poetic, sneakily Strategic-everything Telford writes is also Creatively. Insubordinately Democratic."
—**United States Congressman Hansen Clarke**, Michigan Democrat

"Dr. Telford is a light in these dark ages of education. He is a kids-first visionary who is irrepressible in his pursuit of justice. His Creatively Insubordinate words will resonate to all who dream a better world."
—**Collette Cullen**, author of the play Annie Speaks
(Annie Sullivan was Hellen Keller's teacher)

"*Sensational*-Telford is a real hero to some, a real pain to others."
—**Detroit Free Press**, in an April 18, 2010 review of the author's autobiography (www.AlifeontheRUN.com)

"Still more of John's incisive insights on foiling arrogant autocrats. punctuated with his explosive poetry and sardonic humor."
—**Dr. Wayne Dyer**, world-renowned self-help guru who penned the Introduction to Dr. Telford's book What OLD MEN Know

"An inspiring crusader."
—**Geoffrey Fieger**, Dr. Jack Kevorkian's trial lawyer

"He's *back!* Just when you thought it was safe to pick up a book for quiet reflection. Dr. T. challenges your mind and kicks you in the behind. This isn't a book to be read once and put on the shelf."
—**Dr. Stuart Kirschenbaum**, Michigan Boxing Commissioner, 1981-92

"As always, Telford is as indomitably tenacious as he is insightful, so hold on to your hats-he's at it again!"
—**Robert Landry**, prize-winning artist and sculptor

"From his wild bravado on Detroit's hard-scrabble streets to his lifelong battles with corporate bureaucrats, John Telford now eloquently gives us his Creatively Insubordinate strategies to confound inflexible oligarchs and oligarchies."
—**Fred Lauck**, author of *Children of the Greatest Generation*

"A tragicomic treasure trove of 'Rebelry' that's often less tragic than comic, while offering some Creatively Insubordinate advice that is, in a word-priceless."
—**Professor Robert Leahy**, Stetson (Florida) University

"Creative Insubordination-the title of Dr. John Telford's most recent book-goes a long way toward summing up what this valiant activist-educator has always been all about. The Detroit Board of Education has appointed Dr. Telford to be the interim Superintendent of the Detroit Public Schools. Despite his advanced age, we feel that his expertise, experience, and unyielding dedication to children and to justice for all are a perfect fit for what our school district needs in this time of dire crisis. While his deformational style could rightly be called rather unorthodox at times, his message and some of his methods nonetheless recall magnificent echoes of the righteous revolutionaries of old. Ever since the days when I was a state legislator and he was writing his crusading *Telford's Telescope* columns in the Michigan Chronicle and we joined forces to try to get the Legislature to return to the schools the $220 million in Detroit taxpayers' money that the legislatively-imposed 'Reform' Administration had recklessly and incompetently squandered. I have noted that John Telford is a natural force unfettered by convention and defiant of bungling bureaucracies. If we are

ever to save our schools, our city, our state, and indeed our troubled nation from themselves and from itself. his is precisely the kind of whirlwind force we desperately need."
—**Lamar Lemmons III.** President, Detroit Board of Education

"Dr. John Telford is one of Detroit's best-known critics of the societal scene. He cares fiercely about young people and lampoons inept bureaucrats' craven and uninformed 'leadership. This is a man who 'walks the walk and attacks the mediocrity of contemporary American education and politics. His writing is creative, inspirational, and engaging. Every time this doctor of education puts pen to paper, readers can expect another captivating and insightful journey to a new level of awareness."
—**M. L. (Mike) Liebler,** celebrated poet and editor of Working Words: Punching the Clock and Kicking Out the Jams

"A treasure trove of life's lessons learned from the front lines."
—**Keith Owens,** former executive editor, the Michigan Chronicle

"John Telford is a rebel, a renegade, and a Renaissance man."
—**Huel Perkins,** FoxTV2 Anchor, Metro Detroit

"Cleverly *Creative* and intriguingly *Strategic*. Also, the poems are in turn audacious and heart-wrenching. The Old Master Maverick has penned yet another maverick masterpiece."
—**Robert Plumpe,** Defense Attorney. Team for Justice

"John Telford was born a Righteous Rebel, has lived a Righteous Rebel, and will *die* a Righteous Rebel. In the very early 1960s he was my English teacher and track coach at Detroit Southeastern High School, and like so many of his lucky high school and college students and athletes who have spanned more than five decades. I have remained his lifelong friend. He taught all of us so much more than merely English or how to win races-he taught us advanced courses in Life-and Life is what he continues to teach in this defiantly Democratic and Creatively Insubordinate book. which he has written for us from deep in his audacious and insubordinate soul.
—**Prof. John Powell** of the University of California at Berkeley, former

Harvard Professor of Law and former national legal director of the ACLU

"Acutely sensitive."
—**David Rambeau,** TV producer/host, Project BAIT's *For My People*

"We all stand on the shoulders of righteous crusaders like John Telford."
—**Shawon Respress,** Director of the Opening Gates Residental Care and Treatment Center

"That Telford dude can really *write*!"
—**Sam Riddle,** Insubordinate and oft-publicized Detroit political personality

"John Telford has always stood up for what's right regardless of the consequences. Still, I question whether he's actually truly capable of the more labyrinthine and even sometimes ruthless Strategies he has constructed in this book. Undeniably, they would prove remarkably (and indeed often *terminally*) effective under relevant circumstances. Let me use a bit of the alliteration John himself loves so dearly and top off my testament to his rebelesque rune with these few additional words: I've known John for over fifty years, since we both were 25-and one thing I know for sure is that he's a man of integrity-as well as maybe only *sometimes* Insubordinate!"
—**Rhoda Stamell,** author, poet, professor, and retired teacher of English. Detroit Northwestern and Pershing High Schools

"What John Telford writes, he *lives*."
—**Willie Wooten,** Vice President (retired), Detroit Public Schools Organization of School Administrators and Supervisors (OSAS)

**I dedicate this torrid tome to my lovely and loving wife Adrienne, who was sufficiently *Creatively Insubordinate* to give this now-thrice-married old rogue a third and final chance for blessed connubial bliss.**

It is dedicated as well to all of you Creative Insubordinates out there struggling to right the world's wrongs-and who could use a Strategic snippet of Creatively Insubordinate *support* along the way.

It is also respectfully albeit presumptuously dedicated to those ultra-Creative (although not always ultra-Strategic) C.I.'s alive and dead-namely, the great emancipator *Abe Lincoln*; crusading novelists, columnists and/or journalists *Upton Sinclair, Nat Hentoff, John Steinbeck, George Orwell, E. L. Doctorow. Jonathan Swift, Manuel de Dios Unanue, Rachel Maddow, Han Dongfang, Sydney Harris, Henry David Thoreau, Mark Twain, Joseph Heller, Jonathan Kozol, Bob Woodward, Carl Bernstein, Philip Wylie*, and Egypt's *Aliaa Magda Elmahdy*: Detroit's own activist journalists *Curt Guyette, Charles LeDuff, Sherman Eaton, Catherine Kelly, Valerie Lockhart, Sam Logan, Bankole Thompson, Jim Fitzgerald, Huel Perkins, Larry Gabriel, Zenobia Jeffries, Rochelle Riley, Keith Owens, Cornelius Fortune, Gloria Cunningham, Jack Lessenberry,* and *Diane Bukowski;* social activists *Cornel West, Bernie Sanders, Bill Maher, Lennie Bruce, Cesar Chavez, Albert Shanker, Thurgood Marshall, Gloria Steinem, Eldridge Cleaver, Manning Marable, Danny Glover, Angela Davis, Whoopie Goldberg, Janis Joplin, Buffy St. Marie, Jimmy Hendrix, Lennie Bruce, Mort Sahl, Saul Alinsky, Anita Hill, Rosa Parks, Bobby Seale, Malcolm X, Mae West, Dorothy Parker, Madonna, Jack Johnson, Muhammad Ali, Jesse Owens, Jackie Robinson,* and *Martin Luther King, Jr.*; revolutionary thinkers *Galileo, Martin Luther. Frank Lloyd Wright, Albert Einstein, Noam Chomsky, Reinhold Niebuhr, Andrei Sakharov,* and Wiki-Leaks founder Julian Assange, abolitionists Frederick Douglas and *John Brown;* righteous revolutionaries *Emiliano Zapata, Spartacus, Che Guevara, the Dalai Lama, Mohandas Ghandi (the Mahatma), Nelson Mandela. Mother Teresa* (naturally), *Albert Schweitzer,* Haiti's *Toussaint L'Ouverture,* Burma's *Aung Say Kyi,* Scotland's *William Wallace,* and the United States' *George Washington, Benjamin Franklin,* and indeed *Nat Turner* and *Robert F. Kennedy*: Detroit-area and Michigan activists *John Sinclair,* Mary Ellen Riordan, Herb Boyd, Harry Cook Robert Robinson II, John Percy Boyd. Viola Liuzzo, Malik Shabazz, Agnes Hitchcock, Horace Sheffield,

Jack Kevorkian, Edwin Rowe, John Conyers, Jr., JoAnn Watson. David Rambeau Justin Ravitz, john a, powell (now at the University of California. Coleman Young, Wendell Anthony, Frank Murphy Richard Lobenthal, Delbert McCoy (who overcame being horribly burned), Nicholas Hood III, Barry Ross, Lamar Lemmons III, Kenneth Cockrel, Elena Herrada, Helen Moore, Aaron Gordon, Robert and Judy Wollack, John "Scotty" Telford (my own fighting father), my dad's sister Letty, Yusef Shakur, Hansen Clarke, Keith Johnson, Thomas M. Jones, Jimmy and Grace Lee Boggs, and Corktown priest Solanus Casey; crusading Detroit-area attorneys Bernie Fieger, Geoffrey Fieger, Tom Bleakley, Robert Plumpe, and Frederick Lauck; poets Emily Dickenson, Robert Burns, Pablo Neruda, Nikki Giovanni, Robert Frost, and Carolyn Forché, who wrote achingly of the suffering in El Salvador; fellow Motown-area poets Ron Allen, Melba Joyce Boyd, Aurora Harris, Dudley Randall, Naomi Long Madgett, Karen Dabney, Matt Schatmeyer, Christina M. Brooks, Berhenda Williams, Rosemarie Wilson, Nancy Stevenson, Wardell Montgomery, M. L. Liebler, Ruben Wilson, Angela Nichols, Mildred Williams, Tawana "Honeycomb" Petty. Alford G. Harris; and self-help guru Wayne Dyer (whose home base now is Maui, Hawaii).

Creative Insubordination is lovingly dedicated as well to my own dauntless daughter Katherine Telford Garrett, who once summoned the courage to divorce an emotionally abusive husband, and to her upstanding husband Rich and my cherished grandchildren RJ and Tori, who I trust will one day help create a better world.

I also dedicate it to my 46-year-old son Steven Telford, who, like his father, virtually overcame problematically Insubordinate teen years to emerges creatively (if no longer insubordinately) into the workaday world to contribute his labor for the greater good.

Above all (and most presumptuously of all), Creative Insubordination is humbly. Reverently, and ultimately dedicated to the one undeniably greatest Creative Insubordinate in recorded and unrecorded history-J.C., the all-time, forever time Superstar Himself.

*A*
*Real*
<u>*Righteous*</u>
<u>*Rebel's*</u>
<u>*Resumé*</u>

*I race*
*A fast pace;*
*I read*
*At top speed;*
*I write*
*And I* fight:
*My creed*
*Is to lead.*

Reform
*Is my norm —*
*You need*
*To take heed!*

# CONTENTS

Author's Note .................................................................................. xiii
Foreword by Adrienne Telford ........................................................ xiv
Introduction by Keith Owens ........................................................ xvii

Creative Insubordination ................................................................... 1
    *The Strategies* ............................................................................... 11
    *Terms and Types* .......................................................................... 76
    *A Salient Summary* ..................................................................... 83

The C.I.'s Pop-Quiz Party Games ..................................................... 88

Appendix A - Address of interim Superintendent-elect ................. 118
to Detroit Board of Education, July 12, 2012

Appendix B - Front page, Detroit Native Sun, August 10, 2012 ..... 127
Acknowledgments ........................................................................... 128

Index ............................................................................................... 136
Two Postlude Poems ....................................................................... 142
About the Author ........................................................................... 144

Order Forms
    *Creative Insubordination* ............................................................ 147

# AUTHOR'S NOTE

While on June 14, 2012, the duly-elected Detroit Board of Education paved the way for me to initiate my latest Creatively Insubordinate and egalitarian action by appointing me interim Superintendent of the beleaguered Detroit Public Schools, some Republican legislative and judicial blockage and stalling are currently preventing me from assuming that position (see the Detroit Free Press, June 15, 2012, commenting on my appointment). Indeed, prominent Detroit preacher David Bullock is now warning us, "The rule of law in Michigan is gone. There is no equal protection. We are basically operating at the whim of arbitrary power."

As I will caution you repeatedly in this book, the dastardly Dragon does indeed sometimes win, despite the Herculean oppositional feats of the most Creative of Creative Insubordinates. On July 25, 2012, as this book was going to the printer, the Republican-dominated Michigan Supreme Court stooped to the absurdity of actually debating whether to withhold a challenge to Public Act 4, the state's dictatorial emergency manager law, from the November 6 ballot on the pretext that the font size on the more than 200,000 Michigan citizens' petitions was too small. Should this sort of blatantly partisan judicial blockage and stalling persist right up to and perhaps even beyond the latest date for the quarter-million citizens' democratically signed and delivered challenge to the law to be printed on the ballot, it has the explosive potential to become national news that could foment protest marches and retaliatory action on a national scale. For the future of education and of the revival and survival of Constitutional law in the city of Detroit and ultimately throughout the United States of America, it is to be fervently hoped that this time the Dragon won't win. Only time will tell.

# FOREWORD

by Adrienne Telford, M.A.
—teacher and middle school principal (former), Detroit Public Schools; elementary school principal (retired), Taylor (Michigan) Schools

ONE OLD C.I.'S LEGACY TO HIS LISTENERS

*"The conditions of a solitary bird are five:*
*The first, that it points its beak skyward;*
*The second that it soar to the highest point:*
*The third, that it craves no company, even of its own kind:*
*The fourth that it sing very softly:*
*The fifth, that it has no definite color.""*
—author unknown

When you read this radical book that my grizzled Rebel of a husband has written for you in his seventy-seventh year on this battered old planet, or you listen to one of his lengthy lectures on the liberating process of Creative Insubordination, you will begin to digest some of his relevant activist/ axiomatic Strategies and really hear them with your heart of hearts. You then will recognize your Rebelesque potential for becoming a soaring C.. (Creative Insubordinate), and you will then become fully primed to practice Creative Insubordination (also abbreviated "C.I."-the initials can repr*esent both* the practice and the practitioner).

Practicing C.I. won't make you into a "bird" that "sings softly," of course, quite the contrary. Nor will it turn you into a solitary "bird"--but it will definitely make you a soaring-ly *unique* one, with no distinct or distinctive "color" or "markings" to label or categorize you. The only label that can identify Creative Insubordinates is the glittering "C.I." label they proudly pin on themselves.

Even though my husband's catalytic concept of Creative Insubordination is set in a philosophical framework, C.l. isn't just some maverick method for "interpreting the world." Nor is it merely a means he's offering you to cope with your world, or for simply thumbing your nose at it or even occasionally giving it the proverbial upright middle finger.

Creative Insubordination is a practical process for you to re-create it! This truly cataclysmic concept is going to catalyze you to get yourself prepared to take quick, successful, Creatively Insubordinate (C.I.) action on a billion battlefronts, both personal and professional, light and not-so-light, temporal and eternal. And let me caution you, as he would, with the following blinking lights and sonic speed bumps:

> ***WARNING:* **DANGER** *(Beep!)*
> ***WARNING:* **DANGER** *(Beep! Beep!)*
> ***WARNING:* **DANGER** *(Beep! Beep! Beep!...)*

If you read <u>PAST THIS PARAGRAPH</u>-and if worrying about who's going to judge American Idol next year doesn't rank high among your life's only major concerns you're going to begin to rebel against all the suppressive super ordinates in your life. It's therefore only fair to tell you here and now that this revolutionary book is going to get you Creatively, Insubordinately fired up or maybe sometimes just fired!

Despite what you may have heard about Dr. John Telford or have read about him in the press or in his own newspaper columns or in his books and his poetry, he's really not a totally radical renegade (except when the moon is full). Still, if you've got all the "right stuff" to become a "Real Righteous Rebel." you definitely will decide to embark upon his radically ungentle art of Creative Insubordination after you have taken the time to absorb this tome en Toto.

Once you decide to undertake this art, your life could be changed for ever. That's why it's vitally important for you to understand that while my sagaciously wise yet sometimes un-sagaciously wise-cracking spouse sprinkles in a tongue-in-cheek joke or two (or three or four) here and there, the practice of some of the radical processes found in his Strategies outlined herein actually can involve serious and very real risk. These dangers dictate that not only must you have a good philosophical foundation in C.I.-you must also strategize carefully and creatively before you set about practicing any of them. Otherwise, you actually could very well be fired. Or your lover might leave you. Or you might leave your lover and take a new one. Or whatever! I'm not suggesting that some of these occurrences will or would be completely catastrophic. Throughout your life, there will often be many endings which turn out to be introductions to exciting, new, and far better *beginnings* – as you will also learn in the prescient pages to follow....

# INTRODUCTION

### by Keith Owens
### —former Executive Editor, the Michigan Chronicle

It would take an ultra-philosophical Rebel Sage like John Telford to describe in painstaking detail how being Insubordinate is a wonderfully aware state of higher consciousness to be **aspired** to by anyone seriously committed to promoting the greater good of mankind. After all, this is a man for whom swimming upstream is mandatory.

In the online version of the Merriam Webster Dictionary, the word "insubordinate" is given a distinctly recognizable negative connotation as the most accurate definition of the word to the majority of us who have put that word to use. Most would agree that when one thinks of someone being insubordinate, very few positive images come to mind. More specifically, "insubordinate" in Merriam Webster is defined as "disobedient to authority." As an example given for how the word can be used, we are given two choices:

1. His behavior was unprofessional and *insubordinate*.
2. The junior officer was court-martialed for being *insubordinate*.

In a society such as ours where obedience to authority is next to Godliness. anything contrary to such a mindless state is automatically considered to be in the wrong except by those rare folk such as Dr. Telford, who decided long ago that the very idea of granting authority to an individual simply because that's what the machine requires is sheer lunacy and very possibly suicidal. Without a doubt, a powerful argument can be made that mindless obedience to authority is most likely responsible for a considerable amount of the disasters the world has been struggling through since the introduction of man to the planet.

If Moses was permitted to question the motives of God, then is it really so out of line for us lesser mortals to at least on occasion question the motives of our own bosses in the workplace and elsewhere? Telford's entire life has been a demonstration of just how many ways there are to scream "YES" the only correct answer to this question. And in this sometimes rambling; but perpetually fascinating, entertaining, and instructive book, Telford passes along a treasure chest of life's lessons learned from the front lines.

Lesson number one? Creativity is a must for all those who would challenge the sharp-edged, random whims of authority. A rugged sense of humor doesn't hurt either.

To wit:

> *"For the sake of our nation, I hope to God that President Barack Obama gets a second term. However, if he doesn't, I couldn't care less whether his Republican successor is a fornicating, philandering atheist with an owl fetish or indeed is partial to bonking chickens if he will just eliminate the federal debt, get us and keep us out of war, desegregate the nation, reform the criminal justice system, support an enhanced education budget, engender a genuine green revolution, bring millions of jobs back to these shores, and tame the mega-corporations-and thereby close the income gap between the bloated one presenters and the rest of us struggling or soon-to-be struggling ninety-nine presenters."*

And another one of my favorites, Strategy XXIV:

> *Get rough physically, or threaten to.*
>
> *Being an "old school" educator, when I returned to teach in an inner-city high school on a post-retirement contract in 1999 at the relatively advanced age of 64, I took a recalcitrant and chronically tardy student-an insufferably arrogant star lineman on the Detroit Southwestern High School football team named Tom Chastain-out into the hall, and got Avery Jackson, Jr., Another teacher, to witness what I was about to do. I then removed my glasses and (rather riskily) invited this young football team captain to hit me.*
>
> *Had he done so, he probably would have put me in the hospital.*
>
> *Instead, he said, "Don't wanna."*
>
> *"Well," I responded, "then do you want to do what I tell you to do?"*
>
> *"Yeh."*

> "If I tell you to jump three feet in the air, will you do it?"
>
> "Yeh."
>
> "If I tell you to do it three times, will you do it?"
>
> Hesitation. "Yeh."
>
> "Then go back in there and sit down-and this time, sit in your own seat."
>
> From that day forward, I could do no wrong with that class, nor with that student-who actually began consistently to help me round up some of his tardy classmates, who soon were tardy no longer.

And then there is Strategy XXII:

> **Lie, big-time!**
>
> *Do it boldfacedly, bodaciously, outrageously, intricately audaciously, and flat-out.*

And finally, what I consider to be the nut within the nutshell itself:

> "My egalitarian philosophy has been formed and informed by my experiences as a long-time social activist who has always earnestly endeavored to crusade Creatively and Insubordinately as a public-school and college teacher and administrator and as an official of egalitarian agencies against all forms of suppression (both institutional and personal)."
>
> "Another even more pointedly and essentially relevant key word in this definition is 'Strategic'—since Insubordination that is not strategic perforce cannot be Creative. Creative Insubordination must therefore also necessarily always be Strategic Insubordination."

Now go forth and raise hell. But first read this book so you know how to do it right.

# CREATIVE INSUBORDINATION
## 40 Successful Strategies

**Creative Insubordination (C.I.)** is a strategic procedure that your inveterately Insubordinate old author duly describes as

> The Ancient and Honorable Art of *Radicalized Rebellion*, as practiced by righteously Rebelesque men and women now and throughout recorded history against an obstructive, oppressive, suppressive, de-humanizing
> process,
> person,
> or
> "program"
> within an entrenched "institution."

This institution can be *formal* or *informal*.

It also can be personal or professional.

A key word here is *"entrenched."*

Another even more pointedly and essentially relevant key word in this definition is *"Strategic"*-since Insubordination that is *not* Strategic perforce cannot be Creative. Creative Insubordination must therefore also necessarily always be *Strategic* Insubordination.

An "institution" as described herein can be as complex and Byzantine and Machiavellian as a formally programmed administration, corporation., bureaucracy, or even a *religious organization* or a *national government* whose *entrenchment* has been ensured by tradition and/or by some rigid form of ideology, as well as by powerful special interests.

Nazi Germany and the Soviet Union under Stalin, for example, were two evil archetypical embodiments of the potentially worst elements of such an institution in the twentieth century——the century into which

I was born and spent sixty-four *enlightening* (if often also dismayingly *disillusioning*) years. A third and fourth such embodiment have been this country's Jim Crow laws and its exclusionary real estate covenants. My egalitarian philosophy has been formed and informed by my experiences as a long-time social activist who has always earnestly endeavored to crusade *Creatively* and *Insubordinately* as a public school and college teacher and administrator and as an official of egalitarian agencies against all forms of suppression, both institutional and personal.

Speaking from the institutional perspective, I would suggest that there exist at least some superficial characteristic mutuality's between the monstrous agents of those two historically infamous fascistic archetypes of the century just past and one particular top-heavy and totalitarian urban American school district's top-level and superciliously *classist* officials of my more recent and direct experience–plus some *other* school, municipal, and corporate pseudo leaders I have interacted with or observed whose un-exemplary misbehaviors portend no good for the future of America.

Further, I daresay that there do indeed also exist some characteristic mutuality's between the monstrously deranged leaders of those two infamous fascist regimes of the 1930s and '40s and some of the major players in the Bush II White House of 2000-2008–several of whom belong on death row for treason rather than being suffered to traipse about the countryside making speeches at thousands of dollars a crack. They have helped to put our precious democracy in dire danger of degenerating into an oligarchic *corporatocracy* wherein an elite 1 percent of its citizens possess an obscenely disproportionate percentage of its wealth, and now it is in even greater danger of further degenerating into an absolute *autocracy*-i.e., a *fascist state* whereupon bloody revolution might well become inevitable, as it did in 1776 America against imperial Britain.

We are nearing a cataclysmic era in this country when nearly 99 percent of its citizenry may well encounter extreme difficulty feeding their children by legal means. As we approach this potentially revolutionary era, we have heard, for example, a Republican presidential hopeful named Rick Santorum (*sanctum* Santorum?) tout his familial, faithful "husband-ness" and his seemingly sincere piety as essential qualifiers regarding his fitness for the Oval Office. For the sake of our nation, I hope to God that President Barack Obama gets a second term. However, if he doesn't, I couldn't care less whether his Republican successor is a fornicating, philandering atheist with an owl fetish or indeed is partial to bonking chickens if he will just eliminate the federal debt, get us and keep us out of war, desegregate the nation, reform the criminal justice system, support an enhanced education budget, engender a genuine green revolution, bring millions of jobs back to these shores, and tame the mega-corporations-and thereby close the income gap between the bloated one per centers and the rest of us struggling, or soon-to-be-struggling, ninety nine per centers. It was John F. Kennedy, no less, who warned the world half a century ago, "Those who make peaceful revolution impossible will make violent revolution inevitable," per my following 2012 poem:

*In Dead of Night*

*Erase the "n" from <u>crowns</u>, bejeweled*
*And worn by corporate emperors,*
*You then get pupil-plucking crows*
*Evolved of sable-feathered snakes*
*That flew through prehistoric nights.*
*Therefore beware, O mogul Trump*
*And your <u>own</u> reptilian ilk:*
*It's but one more mis-step down*
*From contemporary night*
*To revolutionary <u>nightmare</u>–*
*And the black and crow-plucked blindness*
*Of the dead.*

(See also The Canine Crusade and Comes the Revolution in the Corollary to Strategy XXXIV.)

Far more *prosaically* and far less <u>*terrifyingly*</u>, an informal (and microcosmic) "institution" as defined herein can also be as basic as-to cite one example a process or practice wherein and whereby a lover and/or spouse is habitually abusive physically and/or emotionally.

Said "institution" can also be as basic as-to cite a second example a process or practice within which some bullying bureaucrat routinely harasses his public institutional or private corporate subordinates by writing them up with petty, stupid reprimands.

It is commonly known that the "good-old-boy" establishment has long been and remains today a well-established "institution" as well. Far too often, many of the proverbial good old boys turn out to be bad old boys-or with increasing frequency, bad old girls like the inept and crony-ridden matriarchy which by 2009 had pushed the Detroit Public Schools beyond the brink of fiscal and academic disaster and thus afforded the Republican-controlled Michigan legislature the opportunity it sought and indeed had happily fostered to hijack and pillage the state's largest school district, a population that is nearly 90 percent African-American.

It should be noted here, too, that one's professional super ordinate sometimes isn't necessarily one's professional superior. He or she may be a highly-placed official's friend or relative, or he/she may have simply been inexplicably dumb lucky to attain the position.

Allow me, then, to creatively and insubordinately split the four infinitives in this sentence to thus express to you that Creative Insubordination (C.I.) also is

> *A continuous commitment to strategically and creatively*
> *Insubordinate you ["ate" rhymes with late-and to*
> *move others toward strategically and Creatively*
> *Insubordination themselves, as well-to any of these kinds of*
> *Institutions, "institutions," or relationships.*

(Quick side-note to Republicans and other Non-Rebels: In the unlikely eventuality that any of you obsequious lower primates are actually trying to read and are even moderately able to read (let alone understand) this Rebelesque Rune, and in the likely probability ja redundancy that you don't own a dictionary please allow me to define infinitive for you. Grammatically, an infinitive linguistic construct containing a verb form preceded by the word "to"-which in other usage is a preposition (but not a proposition, nor does it denote your traditional conservative and presumably customary coital missionary position.) Therefore, the strategically Creative Insubordinate-whom we can also call a Real Righteous Rebel (RRR)-

doesn't hesitate infinitively (and indeed powerful *program, practice, process,* or person *within* it is in fact <u>*oppressive, misguided*</u>, or *significantly <u>flawed</u>.*

He/she also doesn't hesitate to rebel strategically and creatively against our often dehumanizing computerized, internet-fixated, ultra-technocratic environment.

An example of a defiant, Creatively Insubordinate mantra and stance can be fittingly expressed in this pertinent poem, which I call "The Push button Prayer":

> *O Great God Computers,*
> *Compute me some stars.*
> *Construct me a meadow from green isobars.*
> *Produce me a poem.*
> *Present me a brother.*
> *Research me a methodological lover.*
> *Compute me a silver, moon-shimmering sea–*
> *But Great God Computer, pray <u>don't</u> compute **me**.*

My C.I. (Creatively Insubordinate) poem is challenging the computer to do what no mere mortal or mere mortal-generated machine can do or will ever be able to do, no matter how stratospherically soaring the mortal's intellect might be, nor how technologically advanced the machine may be.

Both *social <u>theorizing</u>* and sophisticated *human <u>hardware</u>* do definitely have other uses, however-most of them hopefully being or becoming benignly benevolent. Nonetheless, some of them (both contemporarily and historically) have been and are neither benign nor benevolent:

> *When my dauntless daughter Katherine was fifteen, she creatively and Insubordinately characterized the computerized, impersonal, automated, bureaucratized public institution called "high school" as a hopelessly unsympathetic system run by bumbling, unfeeling bureaucrats. From her perspective (and mine, too, when I was the same age and even at my present advanced age of 76). I have to say that at times this perception wasn't/isn't inaccurate.*
>
> *So as a tenth-grader. Katherine once drew a creatively Insubordinate cartoon depicting a monstrous rectangular wood-and-steel contrivance with a sign on it that said, "Remove the <u>ugly fat</u> from all bureaucracies!"*

*Her malevolently efficient machine was a <u>guillotine</u>.*
I would like to share another Creatively Insubordinate poem with you that I title "Sonnet for a <u>Safer</u> Sea":

*This voyage of historic humankind*
*Is one whereon we're fated to decide*
*If cold creations of the corporate mind*
*Shall specify the way we'll live, or die.*
*We cruise now with mere nautical controls*
*Which navigate us up no harbor path:*
*We try to steer through anti-social shoals*
*With sextants, when we need a sociograph!*
*We automate our elemental selves*
*Computerized, transistorized—yet <u>blind</u>,*
*And thus meander toward unfathomed <u>hells</u>*
*Whence it will prove impossible to find*
*The sort of social innovations we*
*Must seek, to sail upon a safer sea.*

This metaphoric verse takes the philosophical form of a "sonnet for *sanity*," whose rational philosophy all of you righteous reformers and budding Creative Insubordinates out there must urgently embrace for the sake of our warlike, fratricidal species' very survival.

Accordingly, invite you to contemplate yet another relevant metaphorical poem entitled *Rex Reborn*:

*Huger than the heaving ferns.*
*Looming higher than a hill,*
*The thunder thing at night returns*
*To seek and find and pounce and kill.*
*Jungle fires in the night*
*Flicker into spreading flame*
*To cast their blazing, blood-red light*
*Upon the hunter's hiding game.*

*Found, the tiny quarry flees.*
*Teeth like scimitars gleam wet*
*And drip, descending, pierce and seize:*
*The killer gulps and rears erect.*

*Body shining slimy red,*
*Horrid red the staring eye, Tyrannosaurus turns its head*

*To move against the midnight sky.*

*Might once more in fiery glare*
*Over a primeval heath*
*A brute stalk forth to crush and tear*
*And cancel history in its teeth?*

This apocalyptic poem was inspired by the cathartic, soul-searing vision in the poem "The Second Coming," by the prolific Irish poet William Butler Yeats. Similarly to the "shape with lion body and the head of a man" in Yeats' frightful verse, my metaphoric reptilian *Rex* isn't some scary carnivore of eons ago–it's the very contemporaneously "reborn" cannibalistic carnivore of terrorism and corporate fascism and hydrogen bombs and war and holocausts and the Anti-Christ. Even as I sit writing this book, the monster stalks forth again today throughout the world to "cancel *history in its teeth*"-and it must be Creatively Insubordinately halted in its tracks by those Creative Insubordinates among us who care about freedom and about peace with justice.

Here's a fourth short poem that *catharts* on the same unsettling theme:

<u>The Thirteenth Hour</u>

*Xenophobic, ethnocentric, racist, classist kinds*
*Of misanthropically myopic, microscopic minds*
*Mask beneath intolerance a frightful face of fear*
*That's globally infectious–the Holocaust is here.*

And indeed it is.

But now, before I proceed farther in this apocalyptic vein, I need to tell you what Creative Insubordination ***ain't:***

Creative Insubordination ***ain't*** rebellion to be lazy or hostile or chic. Creative Insubordination also ***ain't*** necessarily a process practiced by a subordinate toward a super ordinate on some traditional hierarchical Table of Organization that has lines and arrows pointing up and down to job titles in cute little boxes.

It is vitally important to remember ***this***:

> **The free-flowing, catalytically *strategic* force of Creative Insubordination can flow *down* the Table of Organization and laterally *along* the Table of Organization as well as flowing *up* it.**

Thus, C.I. can be an intensely *grass-roots* phenomenon, as well as vice-versa.

Also, Creative Insubordination can be strategically turned inward upon *oneself* to **pluck out an overweening "super ordinate" personal flaw**, such as situational depression, moodiness, so-called "manic depression" (bipolarity inordinate arrogance, narcissism, egotism, substance abuse, or the tendency to harbor habitual *grudges*, or to play chronic *"blame games"* with friends and loved ones (to offer a few more-or-less common examples here).

For more about the exercise of C.I. upon oneself, I would also refer you to my 2011 book *What OLD MEN Know-A Definitive Dictionary and Almanac of Advice.*

An *athlete, artist, educator, musician, or even a businessman or politician* (to cite just a few of thousands of similarly enterprising folk) can also **strategically InsubORDinate himself herself to any significant obstacle to the achievement of success and indeed to any barrier to the attainment of dominance in the fields mentioned here, as well as in many other wide ranging areas of endeavor, to wit:**

> During my earliest days of intercollegiate quarter-milling in 1954, when I had reluctantly moved up to the grueling quarter from the muscularly equally stressful but ordinarily painless 100-and 220 yard dashes—which were my two most frequent competitive distances in high school-experienced tremendous difficulty "In subordinateing" myself to a physical phenomenon that quarter-milers respectfully refer to as the dreaded "Rig" (short for rigor mortis!).
> 
> The "Rig" is that fearsome python that coils around the thighs and preys on the hearts of long sprinters at a certain point somewhere into the final 100 meters of a 400-meter race and can crush their will and sap their physical ability to thrust and prevail against pain and paralysis and prevent them from winning the race and breaking the record.
> 
> In those early rookie freshman days, the "Rig" would envelop

*and permeate all the muscles in my entire body in the homestretch of an all-out 440-yard or 400-meter dash even when I fancied that physically I was in fairly good competitive condition. At that final stage of the race, suddenly it would feel like I was trying to run on sand, or in ankle-deep water.*

(Note: Long sprinters competing in what I entitled *The Longest Dash* in my best-selling [but now out-of-print] book of the same name also apprehensively call this semi-paralyzing phenomenon *"Hitting the Wall."*)

*Under the guidance of my Michigan Hall of Fame coach David L. Holmes of Wayne State University, I eventually <u>Creatively InsubordinATED</u> myself to The Rig by running several repeat 330-yard intervals at <u>race pace</u> many times in training until I could see nothing but a red haze in front of my bleary and nearly sweat-blinded eyes at the end of those workouts.*
*Thus, my body became accustomed to the leg-lift and reach and the pounding rhythm of running repeatedly at that fierce pace which would need to be maintained for a full 46 seconds under racing conditions.*
*Then in <u>races</u>—even national and international ones— while the ubiquitously intense pain was still inevitably there in the home stretch, with my straining muscles and laboring lungs screaming in vain at my resistant brain to slacken my speed and thus ease off the excruciating pressure on them at least a little the debilitating Rig was reduced to a manageable level. Like the big red record-breaking racehorse Secretariat in the 1973 Belmont Stakes-the third and longest race of the Triple Crown–I was able to InsubORDnate myself to what my agonizing pain was demanding that I do, and instead thrust insubordinately against it and maintain my nearly ten-yard-per second home-stretch momentum all the way to the finish line. I also strategically used Creative Insubordination in quite another way when I was racing a quarter mile. Unlike many of my world-class competitors who were taller, more muscular, and possessed greater sheer, brute speed than I did, I Creatively Insubordinate myself <u>to my own natural impulse to stay with the leaders at the halfway point, which they often reached in 21 seconds or less</u>. I resisted that urge and instead ran the two halves of the race at near-identical speed; e.g., close to 23 seconds for each of the two 220-yard segments of the distance in a 46-second 440-yard race in championship races —where the runners run in their own lanes from staggered*

> starts for the entire distance and thus aren't obliged to bullet out of the blocks and break for the inside lane at a predetermined point on the track (usually at about 180 yards out, depending on the lane). Physiologists have since affirmed that even-pace theory rules in races at 440 yards as well as those at 26 miles (marathons).
>
> Thus, six times I was able to outrun two Olympic 400 meter champions, big George Rhoden of Jamaica and long striding Charley Jenkins of Villanova, and one future Olympic 400-meter champion, muscular Mike Larrabee of the Southern California Striders. All of them customarily tore out and streaked the first half of their race in 21 seconds or better. They would always come back to me, though, in the home stretch—and they were then ripe to be caught, since they had run the first half of their race far too fast.

Nor must Creative Insubordinates always operate *alone*—in isolation *near*-isolation. The wise and strategic counsel of Coach David L. Holmes help me to many a Creatively Insubordinate victory over more physical gifted opponents, as did my 1965 and 1971 book The Longest Dash help can American sprinter Vince Matthews to an even greater and indeed ultimate victory in the 1972 Olympic 400-meter dash—and he said so in his auto biography, *My Race Be Won* (Charter House, New York, 1974, page 96).

During the war of the American Revolution which won our country its independence from the British Crown, it was the legendary inventor, journalist. Creatively Insubordinate insurrectionist, and transcontinental statesman Benjamin Franklin who spoke the memorable line, "Gentlemen, if we don't *hang together*, we most assuredly will *hang separately*." Thus, when necessary, C.I.'s can forge themselves into a formidably numerous fighting force—a *moral* force, to wit:

> In 1993 in Billings, Montana, a bigot heaved a hunk of cinder block through the window of a Jewish family's home that was decorated for Hanukah. A multiplicity of menorahs at once miraculously materialized in windows of Christian homes throughout the entire city. There were a few phone threats ("You're next. Jew-lover," etc.)—but the problem soon disappeared.

Billings, Montana thus proved to be a Creatively Insubordinate community which realized that when one of its families is attacked, all of its citizens are endangered. Billings valiantly and *Creatively InsubORDinATED* itself to ethnic terrorism in the same Creatively Insubordinate insurrectionist mode with which every Dane in Denmark–including the King–defiantly mobilized in great numbers to befuddle the Nazis by wearing the yellow Star of David during World War II when the occupying German Army wanted Danish Jews to wear it so they could readily identify and murder them.

**Who can become a strategically successful practitioner of C.I.?**

*You* **can!**

Even you Republicans can (although many of you seem far less tempera mentally inclined to it). All it requires is simple courage and a willingness to STRATEGIZE *Creatively and imaginatively*, but *cautiously*.

All of this now having been written, let me *induce* you toward and now *introduce* you to some selected Creatively Insubordinate STRATEGIES you might want to use (and a couple you may not want to use) in practicing this most Ancient and Honorable Art:

**Strategy I**

*Conceal* **your insubordinate act from your** *superordinate* **and gamble the he won't find out–or that he will find out too late to thwart you.**

If he *does* find out, tell him he must have forgotten to tell you to do it– or else simply *apologize*. If he is too embarrassed or vindictive to accept an apology, simply hope and pray that your Insubordinate act benefits or will benefit the organization, and that those administrators who occupy executive positions higher than your boss's will take note of that benefit and exonerate you.

(I probably need to point out here that you must always bear in mind that if in being *Insubordinate* you are also unfortunately being insufficiently *Creative*, the Dragon *will win*. Then *you*–as St. George–will fail to free the distressed damsel, who shall then be fated to languish alluringly with the

Dragon in Jurassic Park forever. Meanwhile, the Dragon will devour you piece by-piece, belch sonorously, and then casually pick his teeth with your lance)

> *Between 1995 and 1997, I held a post-retirement position as Manager of Education for an exemplary Detroit-based agency called Wolverine Human Services (WHS) that houses and educates hundreds of delinquent or abused and neglected boys in separate residence facilities. Interviewed and decided to hire a promising young teacher named Mike Oldham, who was a former Rose Bowl star at the University of Michigan and later a wide receiver in the Super Bowl for the Washington Redskins, The director of the residence building where I wished to place this teacher didn't want him and appealed to our mutual super ordinate not to allow me to hire him. Thereupon our mutual boss–who happened to be a close friend of this director–ordered me not to hire the young teacher. I hired him anyway, knowing that the Wolverine Human Services chief executive officer was a dyed-in-the-wool University of Michigan alumnus and sports fan who collected prominent athletes on his staff, and that he would be happy to learn that I had hired Mr. Oldham. (He even sported the U-M block maize "M" in an upside-down inversion as the WHS logo, a "W" for "Wolverine"–the name of Michigan teams)*
>
> *My immediate super ordinate had been boasting to people that he had prevented me from hiring Mike Oldham at the very moment the young teacher was signing a contract with us–and when this super ordinate learned that I had Creatively and Insubordinately effected Mike's hiring, he was understandably embarrassed and angry. Fortunately, Mike proved to be one of our best instructors, and the director who originally didn't want him later told me he was very glad we had hired him.*

*First Corollary to Strategy I*

If your embarrassed and vindictive super ordinate still threatens or is inclined to punish you, make a Creatively Insubordinate counter-threat to reveal some *at-this-point-unspecified* transgression of his to his superiors and/or to the media (whether or not you're actually aware of such a transgression).

## CREATIVE INSUBORDINATION

*Second Corollary to Strategy I*

Tell your super ordinate that you and others are documenting his dictatorial behavior, and then actually *do* document it–and also tell him you're going to organize a coalition bent on his ouster.

*Sub-Corollary to the First and Second Corollaries to Strategy I*

If your super ordinate *does* take unacceptable punitive action, consider the pros and cons of brainstorming alternative counter-strategies with one trusted confidante inside or outside your organization.

Then, if the pros outweigh the cons–that is, if the dangers of not retaliating outweigh the dangers of retaliating–go for it.

*Third Corollary to Strategy I*

Try to enlist inside and outside allies as highly-placed and powerful as possible –both inside and outside the organization-to get your super ordinate to back off.

*Sub-Corollary to the Third Corollary to Strategy I*

If you can, get other lower-ranking but articulate and influential allies within the organization to write letters and circulate petitions supporting you.

*Fourth Corollary to Strategy I*

Let your super ordinate's bosses (and if necessary *others*–including possibly the *media*) know the *whole* story, casting him in as unfavorable a light as possible, or threaten to do this if his action is in the form of an unfair evaluation or a written reprimand based on falsified premises.

*Sub-Corollary to the Fourth Corollary to Strategy I*

In meetings and other public forums, make your super ordinate look as ineptly ridiculous as you can.

*A scathing and sublime example of razor-sharp ridicule that I love to cite comes from the lips of the immortal Creative Insubordinate*

13

> Dorothy Parker. When told that a big-shot bureaucrat was cruel to his <u>inferiors</u>, she inquired, "Where in the world does he find them?")
>
> Parker uttered another famous quip upon her learning of the passing of the laconic, stiff-mannered President Calvin Coolidge. When she heard that he had been pronounced dead, she caustically inquired, "How could they tell?"

### *Fifth Corollary to Strategy I*

If your super ordinate doesn't learn of your act of Creative Insubordination and if long afterward it has proved to be wonderfully productive, risk telling him about it if you think it will cause him to believe that it will make him look good.

You could also try to cause him to think that it was actually his idea. (Were he to realize it was your idea, it could be bad for you, unless you cede him all of the accolades for it. When one is positional subordinate to an insecure and paranoid super ordinate, it can indeed be bad to be good.)

### Strategy II

**Line up support from powerful allies before you perform a justifiably Insubordinate act.**

Then sic these allies on your super ordinate if he seeks to punish you for it.

### Strategy III

**After you perform a necessary act of Creative Insubordination, tell your super ordinate about it when it's *too late* for him to counteract it.**

Then either simply tell him you're sorry or else explain how your innovation <u>benefited</u> the program.

### Strategy IV

**Deliberately *delay* following an order if you know its consequences will be damaging to the productivity or to the elemental well-being of the organization.**

Then carry out the order after it's too late for it to have any adverse effect.

## Strategy V

**If your superordinate gives you a counterproductive order, tell him you *just don't have sufficient time* to carry it out right now, but you will get to it in a week or two.**

By then he may have forgotten about it.

## Strategy VI

**Try always to make your services so valuable to your super ordinate that he'll cut you sufficient slack to *strut your stuff* most of the time.**

This doesn't necessarily demand that you labor sixty hours per week on the job–but it *may*, and it may ultimately even be *worth* it in terms of recognition, promotion, etc.

## Strategy VII

**Prior to committing a Creatively Insubordinate act, make your super ordinate aware of your connections with important and influential people who are either affiliates of legitimate principalities (political, corporate, municipal, educative, etc.) or of illegitimate ones (operatives in variant sub-legal realms who are of various ethnic backgrounds–e.g., southern European, Middle Eastern, African-American, West Indian, Russian, Irish, Albanian, Chinese, Mexican, etc.–you pick it).**

*First Corollary to Strategy VII*

If you don't *have* any such influence, make him *believe* you do, and make him just a little bit afraid you might use it.

If you have a *little* influence, make him perceive it to be a *lot*. And if these "influential" individuals don't even exist, invent them. (As the common truism goes, perception is *reality*.)

*Sub-Corollary to the First Corollary to Strategy VII*

Hint that some of these formidable and familiar friends of yours are, for example, local *Mafiosi*, and drop the names "Vito" and "Big Al" in casual but "confidential" conversation.

In doing this, choose a compulsively gossipy chatterbox of your acquaintance to be your "confidante" whom you know is unable to keep a secret for more than 10 or 20 seconds.

Offhandedly, mention to your "confidante" the fond penchant that your swarthy underworld pals Vito and Big Al enthusiastically manifest for wielding *baseball bats* in environments other than ball fields. Mention also that Vito and Big Al have casually communicated to you on more than one occasion that they would *manifestly enjoy* applying their bats to the kneecaps of your sworn enemies either upon direct request or upon *meaningful suggestion* on your part.

**Strategy VIII**

**Become a high-profile authority in some field other than your primary one– or in your own field but beyond the boundaries of your organization–and make sure your boss and his bosses learn about it.**

If your superordinate perceives that you have this kind of eclectic influence that can give you an independent forum if and when you ever need it, he may be too nervous that you'll use it against him to be inclined to mess with you.

Also, when your super ordinate's *superordinates* become aware that you possess these eclectic skills, it may inspire them to promote you to a position *superordinate* to your *superordinate*! (This happened once in my own career.)

It can also open similar opportunities for you *outside* the organization.

> *In my early years as a high school English teacher in Detroit Public Schools, my former prominence as a world-ranked sprinter at Wayne State University and my then-prominence as a championship high school coach and author of The Longest Dash (the national best selling 1965 and 1971 book on quarter-milling techniques), plus my success as a coach of local champions, gave me ready access to Detroit sportswriters. Occasionally, this prominence helped me fend off super ordinates who made unreasonable, exploitive, or inappropriate demands. (In later years, it also provided me with a ready forum to slip in some sociopolitical and educative commentary.) Champion athletes and championship coaches enjoy perhaps*

> *the most privileged (and also the most misplaced and least deserved) status in schools. Basketball's Bobby Knight's and football's Woody Hayes' habitual spoiled-brat outbursts while coaching at Indiana University and the Ohio State University, respectively, were deliberately overlooked for years by top administrators at those schools who had plenty of reason to be reluctant to reprimand their wildly popular and perennially victorious coaches despite their too-often questionable antics, which included throwing chairs at officials (Knight) and tearing down-markers apart and even physically interfering with an opposing ball-carrier on the field (Hayes).*
>
> *The brouhaha surrounding the unconscionable child molestation involving a coach at the Pennsylvania State University which finally came to light in 2011 would never have been overlooked for so long, had it not been for the popularity and long-time success of Head Coach Joe Paterno and his football regime—a classic but far from unique case of the tail wagging the dog.*
>
> *The famous George Perles-John DiBiaggio incident at Michigan State University in the early 1990s is another and similar example. Perles, the positional subordinate football coach. out maneuvered and eventually bested DiBiaggio, the position ally super ordinate president of the University. When the dust had cleared, the coach had kept the athletic directorship the president didn't want him to keep if he was going to coach football as well.*

What Coach Perles and President DiBiaggio were practicing upon each other was *Creative Insubordination*, pure and simple—but DiBiaggio's brand of C.I. proved less potent than Perles' brand. Perles' influence with the alumni and the board of governors informally cast him as the <u>superordinate</u> despite his formalized *subordinate* rank of coach vis-à-vis DiBiaggio's formalized positional rank of university president.

Also, Mr. Perles was making more money as <u>coach</u> than was Dr. DiBiaggio as *president*. This incidentally is a circumstance which as an educator and as an activist this writer finds viscerally troubling, not only regarding each of these two employees' egregiously imbalanced comparative importance and significance to the missions of their schools, but regarding similarly egregious and pervasive circumstances in *all* of our large universities, and indeed in our *greater society* as well-and I say this forthrightly as a former NCAA All American and world-ranked athlete.

We reward entertainers (and big-time coaches and athletes are in a sense essentially entertainers) far more munificently than we do educators who mold the future of our nation and our world. I fear that one day our nation will *reap the whirlwind* in this regard. (As a matter of fact, it already has, as exemplified by the ascendance of actor Ronald Reagan to the presidency and of athlete/actor Arnold Schwarzenegger to the California governorship)

Those who are familiar with the Perles-DiBiaggio confrontation will recall that President DiBiaggio ultimately and unfortunately left the University when his repeated attempts to pry Coach Perles loose from his athletic directorship proved unsuccessful. Be aware, of course, that in such high-stakes and highly public situations. the reverse could well happen, too:

> *When in the Korean War, General Douglas MacArthur announced his intent to cross the Yalu River into China in defiance of President Harry S. Truman's orders to him to the contrary, the President relieved the General of his command, leading to Mac Arthur's famous retirement speech which featured the memorable words, "Old soldiers never die—they just fade away."*

In a democracy the likes of which the United States still purports to be (rather than the corporatocracy and ultimate oligarchic *autocracy* it has recently manifested some dangerous indications that it could become), its president rather than its supreme military general is by legal decree the commander-in chief of its armed forces. When Mac Arthur, a great general and audacious military strategist but an ultra-arrogant sufferer of the frequently fatal flaw of hubris. Insubordinately (but in this instance *un*-creatively and *un*-strategically) ignored President Truman's direct order, he sealed his own professional and political doom by *overestimating* the extent of his own power and of his influence with the American people and *underestimating* the Democrat President Truman's courage and resolve.

Thus, General Mac Arthur's fellow five-star general, Dwight D. Eisenhower, ultimately ascended to the presidency of the United States on the Republican ticket-a position to which many historians believe the flamboyant Mac Arthur rather than the steady Eisenhower would instead have ascended, had he not *Insubordinately* but extremely *un-Strategically* announced his intent to cross the Yalu river.

Two thousand years earlier, the Roman General Julius Caesar similarly *Insubordinately* but in that historic instance also *Creatively* and extremely *Strategically* did cross *another* river—the Rubicon—in defiance of the powerful Roman Senate. He then marched into Rome with his army in the midst of throngs of cheering Romans, and into timeless history—and had a vast pizza enterprise named for him two millennia later!

## Strategy IX

**If you think your super ordinate is going to give you a bad evaluation on trumped-up charges for reasons having nothing whatever to do with the actual quality of your job performance, go on written record with him before he writes it that you expect it is coming. Also, let him and a few carefully selected others in positions *higher* than *his* know that it is probably coming and let them also know very precisely the real reasons why it is coming.**

In other words, beat him to the punch.

Then if and when the bad evaluation *does* come, you will have neutralized it considerably—and if it *doesn't* come, your preemptive missive may have given him pause for second thoughts and caused him to *decide not* to write it. (1 again writes from personal experience in my citing this Strategy.)

## Strategy X

If you know that your super ordinate wants you gone but can't quite get you out, and your working relationship with him has degenerated to an irreparable point, take a buyout on your terms if and while that option is still available.

### *First Corollary to Strategy X*

Accordingly, as the saying goes, "Let go and let God."

It's often truly heartbreaking to let go, for example, of even a toxic job situation if you have made close friends with some of your colleagues, and if there are parts of the job that you have truly enjoyed. Also, to leave the job is often to feel that you have "surrendered to the Philistines," so to speak–even though you may have lost or given up what was a position of considerable prestige because to do otherwise would have been to compromise your professional and/or personal integrity.

Still, the loss or abandonment of an important job–or, to use a similar example, to be politically passed over for a job for which you are far and away the *best candidate*–can be a devastating diminution of your professional and even economic status. Nonetheless, there are times that after you have done the right thing on the job rather than the *expedient* thing at the expense of your job security and comfort–and ultimately at the resultant loss of the job itself– you do indeed need to "Let go and let God" (even though you may not be particularly religious!).

## Second Corollary to Strategy X

Cathart (ka-THART). Yes, *cathart*! take the lingual liberty of neologizing the word cathart here as the verb form of the *noun catharsis* (and also of *neologizing* the gerundive noun *neologizing*!).

*Catharting* won't ordinarily help you get the job back, but at least when the practice is properly applied, it can make you *feel* a bit better. This is really a form of Creative Insubordination practiced against a destructive internal emotion that has assumed a super ordinate presence within your own susceptible psyche–whether that emotion be situational depression, anger, frustration, etc. – or even murderous rage (see commentary and relevant poem in Strategy XL).

There are many ways to *cathart*, the first and most frequent of them being to "cry on the shoulder" of a staunch friend.

## First Sub-Corollary to the Second Corollary to Strategy X

A second way to *cathart* is to make the <u>media</u> exceedingly well aware of the *superordinate* indifference, ineptness, insecurity, corruption, and resultant <u>injustice</u> of what has befallen you.

# CREATIVE INSUBORDINATION

Do this *gradually*–but continually and aggressively, station-by-station, reporter by-reporter-in each and every local media outlet in the region.

This *second* way to cathart is incidentally a more *externally impactful* way to do it and it is one that I myself did more than once, as described in my 2010 autobiography, *A Life on the RUN* (www.AlifeontheRUN.com).

Often using metaphor to drive my point home, I also did it frequently in my *Telford's Telescope* columns that ran and have run regularly in several news papers in the Detroit metropolitan area throughout the many past years.

Here is an excerpt from one of my *Telford's Telescope* columns that attacked the Detroit Public Schools' matriarchal, inept, corrupt top administration that held sway in the first decade of the twenty-first century. The column was headlined "Job seekers compete under handicap." It appeared in the May 8-13, 2008 edition of the *Michigan Chronicle*:

> *An editorial in this newspaper pronounced Detroit Public Schools a "cesspool of corruption." That it has been indeed–but not only for contract scandals. Its handicap-based promotion process is notorious. As a first-generation Scottish-American. I decided in 1959 to sojourn to Williamsburg, New York to compete in the 440-yard dash at the WNY Scottish Games, only to find that the race would be run on a handicap basis.*
> *Based on my fastest time, I was assigned to run from "scratch" (the full distance). Spread out ahead of me for 70 yards were a dozen runners. I caught the lead runner just before the tape. In my other 173 wins, my competitors ran the same distance I did, but in competing for jobs in DPS, I have had to run farther than the full 440 (metaphorically). In many such "competitions." predetermined "winners" who were given the jobs really didn't race at all. Public employees shouldn't have to compete for promotions on a handicap basis. Both black and white colleagues have said my handicaps are being too white and too old [I was 72 at the time, but my true handicaps have been my skills and my integrity. The incompetent and corrupt don't promote the competent and incorruptible.*

Former State Boxing Commissioner Stuart Kirschenbaum *catharted* similarly in his numerous media interviews after then-Michigan Governor John Engler unjustly dumped him from the Commissionership without a word of thanks for his decade of unpaid and selfless service. A George Puscas column using boxing analogies that was headlined "Firing Kirschenbaum a low blow by Engler" appeared in the *Detroit Free Press* on Wednesday, May 20, 1992. Its opening words were, "Politics in sports can be blind and cruel–and foolish. too. *The best boxing commissioner this state ever had has been knocked out of office by Gov. John Engler.*"

Nobody in Michigan–and nobody in Dr. Kirschenbaum's time *nationally* –performed a boxing commissioner's job with the devotion, intelligence, and effectiveness that were the hallmarks of his administration. Under his direction, Michigan was the state in which drug testing of boxers began and where the Fighter's Passport was developed and made mandatory. (A Passport is a fighter's identification card. Among other items, it lists a fighter's record, with each bout attested to as a fair and legitimate match by the promoter.) Fake records and "ringers" were greatly reduced during the Kirschenbaum administration. and the State Boxing Commission was able to prevent obvious mismatches. Kirschenbaum and his board imposed automatic 60-day suspensions for KO'd boxers. They ordered promoters to put doctors at ringside and ambulances at the door. Dr. Stuart Kirschenbaum almost single-handedly reformed the sport of boxing in the state of Michigan.

Egregiously and incredibly, Governor Engler released this highly competent and effective reformer simply because he had rightly refused to grant a boxing judge's license to a far Right-leaning and politically-connected chap who amazingly was also a self-professed Nazi! This fascistic fellow had appeared in a photograph in a local publication standing beside a large Nazi flag and wearing a military uniform that featured a swastika arm-band.

Dr. Kirschenbaum fought back by *catharting* Creatively and Insubordinately in interviews with dozens of sympathetic reporters and columnists like Puscas. For purely political reasons, Kirschenbaum's *catharting* didn't get his job back. However, it did succeed in bringing down some everlasting and well-deserved criticism upon the head of that politically motivated Republican governor, who was completely indifferent to the dangerous plight of ordinary boxers in the state of Michigan.

### Second Sub-Corollary to the Second Corollary to Strategy X

*Versify!*

Poetry is *art*– and art can often emanate from and be created out of a deep anguish. *Sometimes writing pain-filled verses / To un-cited universes / Can render barely bearable/Unhappiness less terrible.* Thus by means of your own creatively heartfelt poetic expression, you can render yourself *Creatively Insubordinate* to your own *depressed* state. This is therefore yet a *third* way to cathart.

I myself have often *versified* after I have lost or have had to leave a valued and worthwhile job–or when as a result of some fateful eventuality. I lost or had to leave a cherished companion due to divorce or death or some other form of sad separation, e.g.:

<u>A Dirge for Karolyn & Me</u>
<u>And for Me & Gina T</u>

*We bear the messy murders*
*Of our marriages*
*Like leaden burdens laden on our backs,*
*Like scars beneath the surface of our souls –*
*So mourn for Karolyn and me,*
*And for the teeny Gina T*

To write poetry is to make music with words-whether those words and that *music* be lilting and happy or wistful and sad, serene and or tumultuous and angry, metered and rhymed, or unrhymed free verse. Also, you don't have to be a Robert Frost or an Emily Dickenson to write them. It's a wonderful way to retreat into your own little poetic world and close the door behind you to *cathart* in solitude.

Later, if you so choose, you might share your poems with a trusted friend, or even distribute them more widely if they aren't too uncomfortably personal. You might actually wish to publish them in a book, as I have done lavishly and somewhat sneakily herein and in my other books as well (even though much of my poetry is *extremely* personal).

Once you get started, you will be surprised at how good you get.

Here's another relevant example:

### Addiction-Affliction Friction

*I am*
    *a recovering*
*Wanda*
    *holic.*

... and a recovering *Corinna*-holic, and an *Annie*-holic, and a *Karolyn*-oholic, and an *Eva*-holic, and a *Rhoda*-holic, and a *Natasha*-holic, and a *Joanna*-holic, and a *Peg*-oholic, and a *Juanita*-holic, and a *Cecilia*-holic, and a *Katie*-holic. and an *Isabella*-holic, and a *Moniqua*-holic, and a *Monifa*-holic, and a *Gina*-holic, and a *Toni*-holic, and an *Alberta*-holic, et al.-you can fill in your own relevant name or names of the lady or ladies who at some crucial crossroads of your life presumably may have managed to burrow into your very bone marrow (or, depending on your gender: you can write in your own version of an *Addiction-Affliction Friction* poem that you are a recovering *Gino*-holic. or a *Tony*-holic, or an *Alberto*-holic, et al....).

Here are four more examples:

### Something Tranquil

*I found something tranquil*
*Inside and within my*
*Brown sugar-sweet Annie's*
*High tower-top window*
*Thrown wide to the wafting*
*Of winds from the river*
*On sensuous mornings*
*In young throes of spring.*

*I'd slip slickly snug
In her black marble tub
Into hot, wanton Annie's
Warm wetness and softness—
Midst rubbing and cuddling
And bubble and sud.*

*I <u>lost</u> something tranquil
Within and inside my
Brown sugar-sweet Annie's
High tower-top window
Closed tight to the wailing
Of winds from the river
On ever-gone evenings
In old throes of fall.*

**And the second:**

*<u>For Peggy, 1937-2005</u> (written in 2010)
I met a Brooklyn College girl
When I raced in Philly in '55
And fell for her hard.*

*Years passed:
Time and space
And others
Pulled Peggy and me
Ultimately
Apart*

*In 2010,
1 sought her to tell her
That she was in my memoirs:
I found her daughter Jeanne
On Facebook,
And Jeanne wrote,
"John.
Mama's been dead five years—
We should have told you."*

*I'm married now
To a much younger lady
Who's as pretty and bright and brown
As Peggy was.*

> And who has a long and lurid history with me Like Peggy did,
> And who means as much to me
> As Peggy meant—But a Peggy, she isn't.
>
> Yes, time and space
> And others
> Plus this country's
> Crazy race-divide—
> Tore Peggy and me
> Ultimately
> Apart.
>
> Sadly, we
> Never got to
> Have and hold
> Each other
> Ever again,
> Forever.

**And a third:**

> <u>For Katie, 1939-2011</u>
>
> Beautiful musical one,
> You and I
> Were two transitioning trains
> Whose sidetrack couplings and un-couplings
> Kept us from reaching the station together.
>
> It is my deep regret
> My sainted mother. Yet,
> You never ever met
> If there truly is a heaven,
> You and she
> Are right beside each other there

**Here is a fourth example, but with a different twist:**

> I called her "Eva" in my book—
> A flippant filly I forsook,
> Whose flame I finally had to stamp:
> It flared inside her magic lamp,
> Because she was my wild vamp—

*My genie in a bottle.*

*The bottle is gone;*
*Now Eva is calm*
*And serene.*

The "Eva" poem is about how alcohol ultimately ruined a long and torrid romantic relationship (which I also recount in my autobiography, *A Life on the RUN*). Happily for "Eva," her *bottles* now are long gone, but less happily. our passionate <u>relationship</u> is long gone, too.

AC.I. poem can also cathart *exultantly*, so here's yet a fifth little verse I need to insert (if I know what's good for me). I slipped this poem in because Adrienne says a poem about her should be in here, too:

<u>The Third Wife:</u>
<u>Best Is Last</u>
<u>And Last Is Best</u>

*My Adrienne is intellectual.*
*She also is intensely sexual–*
*And yet a halo floats above her.*
*So that is why I truly love her.*

I have one last little *catharting* poem (truthfully, it's only *semi-*catharting) over one of my *long*-ago but short-term and ultra-lustful ladies. It's title: <u>Wanda-lust</u>. However, this particular poem is too "X"-rated for even this audacious tome (and I'm not talking about this <u>Strategy</u> number!).

Also, its *tone* is perhaps too <u>atonally flip</u> to <u>fit</u> here.

However, if some of you somewhat less shockproof souls really want to see this poem, write me at 8900 E. Jefferson, Suit 1107, Detroit, MI 48214 containing your email address and five dollars, and I'll send you a copy if you promise to credit me with its authorship. (On second thought, it's okay if you don't credit me!)

Now let's return to some more seriously *cathartive* poeticizing, because one can even cathart poetically over a lost and torn-down house, if one grew up in it or had nostalgic memories regarding it.

Here's a verse that was featured in the August 17-23, 1988 issue of the *Metro Times*:

<u>Sixteenth Street. 1970</u>

*My spirit in its shallow stream*
*Advanced upon Propitium.*
*Through back alleys,*
*Networked black tunnels,*
*Dark waters,*
*The Low Road flowed*
*Upon Propitium.*

*I sought and found foothold*
*In the house that was gone.*
*The sunshine shone again through empty rooms.*
*(Remember, they had never been her home–*
*Yet I could hear her footstep on the stairs.)*

*A wrecker in a painter's whites stood in*
*An upstairs room, appraising a wall.*
*To hold him from his awful task, I cried:*
*"Would you please paint this scarred and peeling shelf,*
*Or mend this shattered toy?" "No, man," he said.*
*No way"*

One can *cathart* solemnly and self-comfortingly over the loss of long-time *friends*, as well:

<u>On the Passing of Pete Petross</u>

*Superb sprinter, teammate, and colleague:*
*You were the big brother by my side*
*For fifty-seven years– Counseling, cautioning, coaching, cajoling...*

*I only wish that I had listened more–*
*And that I had been able just once*
*To catch you in the hundred-yard dash.*

Ten years my senior, Irving "Pete" Petross, Jr. (1926-2011), was the principal of Detroit's Mumford High School during the increasingly socially turbulent 1980s, when Hollywood star Eddie Murphy filmed a portion of *Beverly Hills Cop* there. Pete shared an office wing with me when we were executive directors together in that same troubled district in the even more turbulent first decade of the twenty-first century. In 1958, he had anchored the Detroit Track Club to a world indoor mark in the four-by-220-yard relay and to a near-miraculous photo-finish silver medal in the national sprint-relay finals in Madison Square Garden after we had *dropped the baton* while in the *lead*, missing the gold by inches! He had also won Michigan AAU sprint titles a record five times.

Here's another one:

> <u>For My Lithe and Legendary</u>
> <u>Wayne State University Teammate</u>
> <u>Cliff Hatcher, 1933-2006</u>
> *Forty-eight and eight-tenths of a second.*
>
> That's how long it took you sixty-one years ago
> To shatter the Motown mark in the 440-yard dash
> And become a stellar member
> Of the 1951 All-American high school team.
>
> *Two years later*
> *As an aspiring high school record-breaker,*
> *I read your incredible time in the record book*
> *And hoped it* <u>had</u> *to be a* <u>typographical error.</u>
>
> *On a high school track*
> *You were an amazing, blazing,*
> *unbeatable brown blur.*
>
> *When thanks to your inspirational role-modeling*
> *I became an NCAA All-American*
> *And presumed to outrun you a few times.*
> *I felt like* <u>apologizing</u>.
>
> *Throughout the ensuing half-century,*
> *You were to remain my hero,*
> *My mentor, my best friend,*
> *And the stellar member*
> *Of my own personal lifetime,*
> *All-time, All-American team.*

(Cliff died more than five years ago, but still misses him fiercely–we ran together on many a championship relay team, and we hung out at each other's houses nearly every week for fifty-two years. He was the best man in my first wedding. I was married in his manse in Detroit's elegant old Sherwood Forest subdivision in my ill-advised second, and I am godfather to his darling daughter Joy.)

Here are two other poems expressing shock at sudden passing:

*Ode to Giovanni Scavo*

*In 1957, in summertime Bologna,*
*Upon \*Reunione Internazionale.\**
*I defeated Scavo in the \*\*quattro-cento metri.\*\**

*I was twenty-one; he'd just turned nineteen–*
*\*\*\*Atletica Leggera's\*\*\*\*\*\*Enfante Il Terrible!\*\*\*\**

*Before the race, the sold-out crowd*
*Had chanted "<u>Scay</u>-o!" really loud.*

\*Pronounced ray-YOU-nee-<u>OH</u>-nay EEN-tair-<u>NASH</u>-eeoh-<u>NAHL</u>-ay-eleven syllables
\*\*400 meters
\*\*\*Atletica leggera is Italian for "track & field"
\*\*\*\*Pronounced Ain-FONT-ay eel Tair-EE-blay


*Afterward, we traded pins*
*And promised that we'd write:*
*Came this letter, two months later–*
*From Italia by slow freighter*
*"John and Gio run one-two in*
*Rome Olympics, 1960!"*

*Just before, I'd read he'd driven*
*Fast and far in his Ferrari*
*From the famed Eternal City*
*Toward the reaches of the Marches*
*Near the heights of the Abruzzi,*
*Crashing high up on a mountain–*
*And there died in his Ferrari.*

*Italia mourned her \*\*\*\*\*campione\*\*\*\*\*–*
*The champion runner, Giovanni.*

\*\*\*\*\*Pronounced KOM-pee-OWN-ay

Incidental note: Giovanni Scavo's countryman Livio Berruti, then nineteen as well (and against whom I had also raced) went on to win Olympic gold in Rome at 200 meters in 1960, sporting his trademark sunglasses and gold chain, defeating both of the American finalists in a huge upset.

The other poem reflecting shock contains sad news I have just now received on May 9, 2012 even as I write:

<u>*Frank Carissimi, the Denby High Flash*</u>

*From 1958 to '60,*
*I coached the speedy young Carissimi,*
*Who ran the fastest metric mile*
*Of any boy in a long while.*
*When Frank was a fresh and irascible teen,*
*His drugs and divorce and his stroke weren't foreseen.*
*Today from his daughter I get this dread call*
*That casts on my numbly stunned mind a dead pall.*
*In near disbelief and incredulous grief*
*I whisper the paraphrased words of a chief*
*By the name of MacArthur–his final goodbye:*
*"Old champion <u>milers</u> don't ever just die–*
*They speedily fade away, up in the sky."*

One can also cathart achingly over the irrecoverably debilitating loss of cherished family members or over traumatic contretemps involving cherished family members:

<u>*For My Big Blond Cousin Carl 1935-2003*</u>

*You– and your hero-soldier brother Dick–*
*Were bred of valiant Viking Norsemen stock;*
*Mix in that dauntless dash of DNA*
*To the genes of the son of a brawler Scot:*
*The product thus was three braw Musketeers,*

# CREATIVE INSUBORDINATION

> *Cousins closer even than brothers be.*
> *Proclaiming all for one and one for all*
> *Throughout those 1940s green and gone*
> *In rustic rural redneck Royal Oak,*
> *And then throughout the 1950s days*
> *In muddy olden DEE-troit Motor-Town.*
>
> *One afternoon in 1959*
> *We warned three drunken hoodlums not to curse*
> *In front of some old ladies in a bar—*
> *The beery trio followed us outside*
> *To jump us both inside the parking lot.*
>
> *One sucker-punched and kicked me in my head*
> *And grabbed my hair and kneed me in my nose:*
> *You sent him bleeding from his mouth and ear*
> *With his pair of likewise battered friends*
> *To keep me bashed and bloody company*
> *Within the St. John Hospital nearby.*
>
> *My cousin-brother, I could count on you!*
> *I miss you always—every single day.*

And another:

> <u>Unstarlit</u>
> (written for my shy, sweet cousin Janet, who died at nineteen? in a roller-skating accident in 1953, when I was seventeen)
>
> *She liked the spring the least of all—*
> *Because it promised, passed; soon fall*
> *Appeared in summer's dust–the gall*
> *Of spring's sweet testament gone sour*
> *Remained in fall. Her favorite hours*
> *Passed promise-less—white winter hours*
> *Which pledged no green consents to be*
> *Unkept. She wished she mightn't see*
> *Another May. Unhappy, she*
> *Remembered desperation, pondered*
> *Brutalities observed, and wondered*
> *When lines of long horizons ended.*
> *Her Junes had been one joyless ark*
> *Of burning days; then humid, dark,*

*Lake-palmless, gray amusement parks*
*Her Augusts. Lights illuminated*
*But couldn't brighten oddly faded*
*Unstarlit, Ferris-wheel-jaded*
*Disinterested faces—when*
*One fall, an unremembered glen.*
*Well-sheltered from the face of men,*
*She found again.*

And another:

<u>*My Silent Violin:*</u>
<u>*Un-played Then for Scotland-Born Dan –*</u>
<u>*The Uncle I Dinna Ken –*</u>
<u>*And Indeed Never Knew*</u>

*Danny Boy.*
*They wouldn't let me play your song*
*In the old frame house on 12th Street*
*Where you killed yourself over her.*
*Even decades later,*
*No one could ever even say your name*
*Without your sisters starting to cry.*

*As I write,*
*You're staring blindly out at me*
*From your big colorized picture*
*On its 1920s-era stand –*
*You were a good-looking lad,*
*Like your brother, my dad.*

*Once they mistook him for you*
*Sparring in the ring at Silman's:*
*But you were taller—and unlike him,*
*You wouldn't hurt a fly.*
*I'm told you caught spiders*
*And put them outside:*
*We have that in common.*

*I viscerally wish that somehow*
*You could tell me*
*If she was really worth it.*

*(But even though you can't.*

*and even if she wasn't,*
*I still can empathize.)*

And another:

<u>The Crushed Flower: An Anomaly?</u>

*When my darling daughter was nine,*
*She crushed a flower in a paper cup*
*belonging to a little girl visiting grand-folks next door.*
*I then hastened however*
*to reassure myself*
*That this cruel crushing had to be a mere anomaly,*
*Rather than a fey foreshadowing*
*Of my daughter's adult persona.*
*Today I forlornly endeavor*
*to so remain reassured,*
*Because whatever headstrong contretemps*
*we may cause to come between us –*
*whether rightful or wrongful,*
*past or present.*
*fair or unfair–*
*She shall be and shall have been*
*unto and beyond my death,*
*My deathlessly, deathlessly darling*
*Daughter.*

And yet another:

<u>For Tori</u>

*My daughter's*
*Daughter's name*
*Is tattooed on*
*My daughter's skin–*
*And o n my soul.*

In the latter poem. I *cathart* over a granddaughter who nevertheless is actually and thankfully very much alive–and is, in fact, three years of age, but some temporary circumstances have prevented me from being able to see her and her 6-year-old brother RJ nearly as often as I would like to.

I now seek to inflict just two more (mercifully *brief*) cathartive verses upon you.

The first is about my sometimes somewhat strained relationship with my 45-year-old son, and the second is about the grandfather he never met:

*For Steven D. Telford*

*I sired a son with another man's wife.*
*The other man had him for half of his life.*
*Now I and my son suffer struggle and strife*
*That cuts and can stick and stab deep as a knife –*
*But I gave him my home to live in,*
*Because he is my son..*

*Our bonding may wane and our pain remains rife.*
*With ongoing strain and great struggle and strife*
*That cuts and can stick and stab deep as a knife–*
*But I give him my <u>heart</u> to live in.*
*Because he is my son.*

And:

*For Scotty: A Caledonian Canticle*

*My daddy didn't die where he was born–*
*Larkhall, whence ancient kin rode forth on raids*
*Or got well-bled at Culloden*
*Or torn at bloody Bannockburn by English blades.*
*A-gasping, gang aglie.*
*"Dear Mother. I die free!"*
*No.*
*He died one drab,*
*inconsequential day*
*On some gray bed in distant Michigan –*
*A billion heartbeats and a world away*
*From Highlands where the sons of warriors ran*
*By bright burns blue and clear,*
*Chasing dew-dappled deer.*

(Note: This poem was inspired by the poem My Heart's in the Highlands by Scottish poet Robert Burns, who was born January 25, 1759, one hundred and seventy-seven years before this aspiring first-generation Scots-American versifier was coincidentally born on Burns' birthday.)

Now, back to the Strategies!

**Strategy XI**

**Use the media *openly* and in an *IMMEDIATE BLITZ* if the situation is urgent.**

(This Strategy has also been exemplified in the more moderate and long-term application in the second *catharting* in the First Sub-Corollary to the Second Corollary to Strategy X, preceding, that described the masterful way in which then-State Boxing Commissioner Stuart Kirschenbaum did this.)

Absolutely do not *hesitate* to resort to and call upon the media *at once*– if, for example, you have venal corporate or academic bosses or a nervous governing board that has put you under a gag order for some righteous but controversial action you have taken.

Do this to *whatever extent* this may be necessary and possible.

In fact, if you are able, do what I did more than once under this circum stance, which was to call a prompt *press conference* and also make an immediate string of appearances on local television and radio shows–and then have my friends outside the organization write letters to newspaper editors supporting me and castigating my super ordinats for the action they sought to take against me, as Dr. Stuart Kirschenbaum did so masterfully as described in the First Sub-Corollary to the Second Corollary to Strategy X.

In one situation, I was also able to have the national legal director of the ACLU– a former student of mine–write a letter to my board president advising him that if he were to dare to touch a single hair of my hard little civil-libertarian head, the entire legal apparatus of the ACLU's national office would be put at my disposal *gratis*, to fight my firing.

Also and again– and similarly to– the Sub-Corollary to the First Corollary to Strategy VII, now give you a

*Corollary to Strategy XI*

Blab *strategically selected* portions of your predicament to the *biggest gossips* you know, and also march, picket, and demonstrate.

A superordinately imposed gag order is for your *superordinate's* benefit—certainly not for *yours*. If you remain silent, it becomes much easier for him/her to subordinate and subdue you-and even to *fire* or *expel* you.

I could offer many illustrative stories relevant to *Creatively Insubordinate Strategy XI* and its Corollary from my own personal experiences (as well as some illustrative ones relevant to Strategies IX and X). I do recount some of them in my 2010 autobiography. *A Life on the RUN – Seeking and Safeguarding Social Justice* (www.AlifeontheRUN.com) and in *What OLD MEN Know*, my 2011 *Definitive Dictionary* and *Almanac of Advice* (www.HarmonieParkPress.com). However, I like this one that exemplifies Strategy XI even *better*:

*Top administrators at the University of Maryland ordered demonstrating professors and students to take down their American flags and other supportive symbols of our soldiers fighting in Operation Desert Storm in the Persian Gulf War in 1991. Also, staff members were ordered not to talk to the media about the situation. The administration said they issued this order because they had a "broadly diverse" population (translation: lots of Arabs) to be sensitive to, and what might appear innocently inconsequential to one person could be insulting to another.*

*When the demonstrators got the story into the student newspaper and the Washington Post, the administrators did a fast and predictable about-face, proclaiming that they strongly supported such displays in the good old All-American spirit of freedom of speech, etc., blah-blah-blah....*

## Strategy XII

**If a bullying superordinate or other hostile individual threatens you during a phone conversation, tell him to talk a little louder so your (imaginary) tape recorder can pick it up.**

He'll hang up in a hurry. (Or else, really tape him and warn him afterward that now you have a tape which the media and the central administration would find to be of more than passing interest.)

> *Several decades ago in Detroit, a high school athletic director who envied the popularity of his head football coach was plotting to fire him. The coach's friend and erstwhile fellow coach who had been transferred to another high school and was coaching track there had been made aware of this via telephone calls from former students and athletes at his old school, and he began to mobilize them to save his former colleague's job.*
>
> *When the athletic director's high school principal furiously phoned the young coach and told him he would "get him" if he didn't keep his nose out of the situation, the young coach did indeed duly invite the principal to "talk a little louder" so his (actually imaginary) tape recorder could pick it up-and the principal did indeed hang up in a split-second-quick hurry.*

Incidentally, in that situation, the popular head football coach's job was saved-and the fortunate fact that his team won the city championship that fall ensured its salvation. I have said many times that there are few jobs in all creation that are safer than the job of a winning athletic coach.

**Strategy XIII**

If despite your maverick nature you've miraculously managed to attain a top executive position within a bureaucracy, use your position-power to be Creatively Insubordinate in positive and productive ways which before had perhaps been difficult to pursue.

This Strategy obtains if the bureaucracy you've become an integral and highly placed part of is indeed in significant *need* of reforming and if you really want to reform it and are willing to risk and to dare to effect this reformation.

This Strategy also obtains if there are persons within the bureaucracy who need to be reformed or neutralized:

> *In the early 1980s, a Plymouth, Michigan parent named Mary McGrath appealed in desperation to the Plymouth/Canton School District's Executive Director of Secondary Education who she had heard had a record of bucking the teachers' union, the Super intendent,*

*and the school board when he felt it was necessary to do this in the better interest of a student or students.*

*He was, in other words, an occasionally Creatively In subordinate as well as a Creatively Insubordinate super ordinate.*

*Ms. McGrath's extremely intellectually gifted but also extremely bored and chronically truant daughter Coleen had been retained in the ninth grade twice and had been tossed back and forth like a hot potato between three different junior high schools within the district. About to be retained a third time and transferred yet again, this gifted girl was threatening to quit school.*

*Overruling this committee decision of the principal, a social worker, a psychologist, and a teacher, the Executive Director <u>enrolled her in summer high school French and Algebra</u> with the stipulation that if she excelled in those classes, he'd promote her in the fall, via administrative fiat. She got an "A" in French and a "B" in Algebra: He promptly advanced her to the tenth grade over the overruled committee's vehement protest.*

*The gifted and academically under-challenged Coleen McGrath graduated from the high school and ultimately from the University of Michigan with honors instead of ending up flipping burgers forever in some roadside fast-food establishment.*

*For many years afterward, young Miss McGrath sent Christmas cards to the Executive Director, but he has since lost touch with her.*

### *First Corollary to Strategy XIII*

Once you have attained this level of power, then Creatively and Insubordinately dare to share some of it. Set up a suggestion box and act on the most meritorious suggestions.

Thus, instead of trying to beat down a creditable insurrection of Creative Insubordinates, you join it from above as the super ordinate!

Trust me– rank-and-file workers on the front line, whether they be teachers. custodians, salespersons, or whatever-know a whole lot more than many other folks (often including their bosses) would ever imagine about how to run the organization; or if it is a school district, about schools and schooling.

## CREATIVE INSUBORDINATION

### *Second Corollary to Strategy XIII*

Consider letting your subordinates evaluate their super ordinates-including you.

(As mentioned in *A Life on the RUN*, I actually pioneered such a process when I was the Deputy Superintendent of Schools in the Rochester [Michigan] Community School District, and if you write to me requesting it, I would be more than happy to email you my sample matrix for this.)

Should you be bold enough to initiate such a democratic process, your administrative credibility will deservedly *soar*. (You may also have to fend off a grievance from your unionized subordinate administrators—and that's one of many other personal experiences I may decide to take the time space to describe in a sequel memoir to A Life on the RUN.)

### Strategy XIV

**If you think your position is strong enough, or if you feel strongly end about it, and your stance is righteous (and sufficiently desperate), be <u>*openly*</u> Insubordinate.**

Do this even if it involves breaking a *rule*– or in extreme circumstances breaking a *law*, if the rule is ridiculous, grossly inconveniencing to the is imposed upon, or it is likewise unfair, or if the law is unjust, e.g.:

> *Mark Twain's natural-born Creative Insubordinate Huckleberry Finn broke an unjust law that legitimized the immoral institution of slavery when he harbored and hid the slave Jim from the sheriff.*

Here's an additional example:

> *In 1964, a young English teacher in a then all-white Detroit high school taught a unit on brotherhood that he had written as his essay for his master's degree in English Education. Parents of some of his students called the principal to protest that he was teaching their offspring to "love Negroes." The principal ordered the assistant principal to tell the young teacher to cease and desist from teaching the unit.*
>
> *This the assistant principal then dutifully did. He also advised the young teacher that brotherhood "<u>has nothing to do with English</u>."*

# CREATIVE INSUBORDINATION

*The young teacher, who had just been deservedly and by the great grace of God granted tenure, disobeyed the assistant principal's order and somewhat surprisingly, there were no unpleasant consequences whatever for the young teacher. The building administration backed off, looked the other way, and let him teach his beloved Brotherhood Unit to his heart's content and to the lastingly egalitarian educative benefit of his students.*

*(Ironically, this assistant principal, who was himself a member of an often-persecuted minority group— he was Jewish— was rather remarkably <u>promoted downtown</u> to a position of "<u>intercultural coordinator</u>"!] soon thereafter, One can only wish that his experience with the young teacher and the brotherhood unit had a salutary and reformative effect upon him— and one also can only hope that he did indeed become reformed, rather than remain a rank hypocrite.)*

Here's a third example:

*Some years after I had retired from suburban school administration, and had returned to Detroit Public Schools—where I had begun teaching and coaching in the 1950s; I was teaching and coaching track and cross-country at Southwestern High School. The year, incidentally, was 1999. In the fall of that year, I was told that for reasons of district liability, I had to take my cross-country team to a particular meet in an expensive taxpayer-paid bus, even though I had only three runners competing in that particular meet. <u>I nevertheless canceled the bus and took the three of them in my car against orders</u>.*

*Later in the semester when I wanted to take four of my journalism students to the Detroit Free Press building, I was told to <u>take them in my car</u> (which I did)! Go figure.*

## Strategy XV

**Slip some *administratively time-consuming* obstacles into your super ordinate's path now and then.**

He'll then become too bureaucratically busy to meddle in your leave it to you to think up some ways to do this, since you're familiar with your own job situation and with the possibilities for appropriate examples activities. I of such obstacles, and for the means to put them in place, and I'm not— which leads us smoothly into my next Strategy:

## Strategy XVI

**Periodically, leave a few very *intricate* strings untied just before you go on vacation or before you take some personal or sick days.**

These strings should be difficult ones that only *you* have the information and expertise to tie without instructions or counsel. Then remain *incommunicado* when your super ordinate bombards your answering machine with frantic questions.

Finally, come to his rescue like Captain Justin Tyme leading the cavalry coming over the hill with a return call to him *at the very last minute* with the answers that will enable him to circumvent or overcome the difficulty.

A crisis like this will make you appear so indispensable that later your super ordinate may compromise and give you your way on some pivotal issues even when he disagrees with you.

(It also may get you reprimanded or fired if you bungle it. The key word here is "difficult" as distinguished from "vital.")

## Strategy XVII

**Find creative ways to subvert *unfair*, time-expensively *inconvenient*, or preposterous rules or laws.**

There are some officiously bureaucratic super ordinates that would likely follow an absurd directive in a memo to them from their super ordinate even were it found to contain– and to be the *result* of– a *typographical error*, and they would expect you to follow it, too. (Such bureaucrats [bureau-*rats*?||] unquestionably would make <u>*excellent*</u> Nazis.)

Again, I'll leave it to your discretion to devise pertinent ways to "tease" your super ordinate and simultaneously circumvent some of these rules, since you know your situation and don't. However, I will give you a few examples.

Here is one from my own experience and one in which I mischievously chose to be a petty irritant, a sort of "psychological gadfly":

## CREATIVE INSUBORDINATION

> When I was a young teacher of English, had a department head who insisted that all of the teachers in his department read reams of pedagogical data that he posted on his office bulletin board every morning and sign their names on a sheet on the board as proof that they had read it. When I began repeatedly to neglect to sign his sheet, he kept putting notes in my office mailbox order ing me to resume signing it, so I had a colleague sign it for me every morning with the stipulation that he was never to tell me what was on the board. (I incidentally was never the worse for not knowing what was on it.)
>
> After I had transferred to another school in the district to teach English and coach track there, my colleague– a truly great teacher named James Campitelle– whimsically continued to sign my name to the bulletin board.
>
> (In those days, Jim and I also were immature enough to invert a student we named "Waldo Pond" and keep marking "Waldo" absent. After "Pond comma Waldo" began to appear regularly on the absence lists, we got Waldo a report card and gave him all A's. If I had remained at that school, perhaps we could have got Waldo graduated summa cum laude and secured for him a scholarship to Harvard, because insofar as we knew, no administrator or counselor ever checked up on the wandering Waldo.)

Here is another example, initiated by an old acquaintance of mine:

> A skilled potter who sold pottery out of her Rochester Hills, Michigan home, Helen O'Neill routinely advertised her wares in her front yard via signage next to her roadside mailbox. When City Hall ordered Ms. O'Neill to stop advertising in this manner because it violated a bureaucratic municipal regulation, she legally (and creatively insubordinately) <u>changed her name</u> to Helen O'Neill Pottery!
>
> She then painted her new surname in large letters on her large mailbox. Bureaucratically-imposed problem solved.

Here's another:

> In 1994, the authorities in Lauren, Iowa, ruled that a 73-year old resident named Alvin Straight was too old, infirm, and weak vision to be allowed to have a driver's license. In August of that year, Alvin's 80-year-old brother Henry who lived two hundred and forty miles away in Blue River. Wisconsin had a stroke, so Alvin Creatively and Insubordinately drove his tractor-which didn't require a driver's license

43

> *the entire two hundred and forty miles to visit his ailing brother.*
> *The trek took six weeks.*

## Strategy XVIII

**Rather than rock the boat, rock in the boat.**

> *Nationally renowned educator Fenwick English once told the tale of the young rookie curriculum coordinator who was enthusiastic about an innovative concept called "curriculum alignment" and wanted some tough old birds on a high school teaching staff to try it. So she didn't call it "curriculum alignment." Instead, rather than couching it in educationist terminology that these traditional old teachers held in often fully understandable contempt, she called it simply "strengths" and "areas needing improvement."*
>
> *Presto! Her barnacle-encrusted old birds accepted it without the usual griping about "new-fangled fads," etc. She had slipped them some Creatively Insubordinate new wine in an old bottle.*

This also brings to mind the example of one of my very resourceful and Creatively Insubordinate young principals in Rochester, Michigan, where I was the deputy superintendent in the 1980s and early 1990s:

> *Hart Middle School Principal Tresa Zumsteg was having trouble getting her staff to come to meetings on time. To solve the problem, she put out shrimp dishes that would serve only about eighty percent of them.*
>
> *The on-time staff members ate delicious shrimp; the late ones didn't get any.)*

## Strategy XIX

**If traditional methods don't work, try something radically and Creatively Insubordinately <u>un</u>traditional, as this Nevada couple did in the year 1992:**

> *When the landing gear on their small plane wouldn't open due to lack of hydraulic fluid, Steve and Kathy Swigard urinated copiously into the machinery–and the gear came down!*

Another similar example, which shared in part with you earlier:

> When I was a nascent quarter-miler in the 1950s, I started out rocketing the first half of my races nearly all-out in time approaching 21 seconds, and I would find that in the home stretch I had little fuel remaining in my tank to burn against national-class competition. I decided to experiment with the then-revolutionary concept of even pace for long sprinters: With considerable psychological difficulty, I forced myself to hold back and run my first 220 yards slightly under 23 seconds, rather than running it slightly over 21 seconds-and then I came back with a second 220 close to 23 seconds instead of in a fading 26 seconds.
>
> In that fashion, I became able to run faster than 47 seconds for the entire 440 yards and indeed did outrun 1956 Olympic 400 meter champion Charley Jenkins of Villanova University in the 1957 NCAA 440-yard dash final in equivalently faster time than he had clocked winning the Olympic title. Using that same even pace technique, I outran him again the next week in the National AAU Championships, earning a berth on the United States team that toured in Europe, where I went undefeated at 400 meters.
>
> Ultimately, I wrote my anecdotal techniques book, *The Longest Dash–A Running Commentary on the Quarter Mile*. Touting even pace in the book, and as I proudly mentioned once in here already, on page 96 of his autobiography, *My Race Be Won*, 1972 Olympic 400-meter champion Vince Matthews of the United States credited my book for his upset victory in Munich in the 400-meter dash.

Incidentally, that book of mine on the quarter mile, which was published by Track & Field News Press, sold out in two editions–1965 and 1971-and is now out of print. My Cousin Jeff Telford's son Jeff Jr. says he saw it advertise recently on Amazon for eighty dollars. In 1965, its original price was one dollar!

## Strategy XX

**File a grievance against your super ordinate-or threaten to.**

Throw in any vaguely relevant charge you can think of which might apply even remotely: sexual harassment, racial discrimination, age discrimination everything but the kitchen sink.

Remember, Creative Insubordination at this stage becomes all-out warfare—and you can definitely forget about expecting your super ordinate to fight fair. It never ceases to amaze me how the threat of grievance or suit can buckle the knees of even the most brutish of bullying bureaucrats (particularly if such action might be publicly embarrassing to him).

Remember this, too:

All *bullies*-whether or not they be bureaucrats– are basically <u>cowards</u>.

**Strategy XXI**

**Threaten to sue your superordinate– or to sue the company.**

I myself was sorely tempted to sue one particular large urban school district that had terminated me from two executive directorships and one curriculum coordinator job– *once* for criticizing asinine decisions of the then-chief instructional officer, once for whistle-blowing regarding inept, high-handed and corrupt practices at top levels, and once for neglecting, due to illness (kidney stones), to take required course-work in courses I easily could have taught.

The district's top administrators had also turned me down for positions for which I was immensely overqualified, and I had proof that at least one of those rejections was verifiably age-*discriminatory*.

(It is significant to note here that when I was the curriculum coordinator and instructional leader in that district's toughest high school between 2003 and 2008 and I was also *teaching* there, an award-winning young film-maker named Oren Goldenberg came and filmed me in my classroom for a documentary he was making on the schools and on me and longtime fellow Detroit activist Grace Lee Boggs, age 96.

After only one day of filming, the central-office honchos downtown found out he was interviewing me and some of my students. They immediately called the principal and ordered him not to let young Mr. Goldenberg film me on campus. (Part of that film is currently on YouTube and can be tuned in on my website, www.AlifeontheRUN.com.)

I was aware that almost all of the petitioners who *did* sue that woefully mismanaged district won their lawsuits, but I had been educated in the district from kindergarten through twelfth grade, and I just couldn't bring myself to sue it despite my young second wife's vehement urging. To me, it would have been like *suing my own mother*.

> Shortly after I retired from public school administration, the director of the Metropolitan Detroit Youth Foundation recruited and hired me as his executive deputy director. At his invitation, I took up residence in my new office, purchased two expensive new suits, had cards printed, and made the rounds of the offices of my influential friends and contacts who could help the MDYF get out if a deep financial ditch which had been dug by thieving and high-placed former employees.
>
> Presently, one of the organization's board members decided he wanted my job for himself, and the director informed me sheepishly and apologetically that he was going to have to un-hire me. As you can imagine, this didn't sit very well with me. I sued, won, received a fair monetary settlement, <u>and made sure that the media covered my successful suit</u>.
>
> The agency unfortunately closed its doors soon afterward. I was one of the only litigants to collect from them, because very soon thereafter no money remained in the defunct Foundation's coffers to pay any of its creditors. It had all been squandered or stolen, and one particular executive of the organization was sentenced to serve a considerable amount of prison time.

(For more elaborate details regarding this lawsuit, see Strategy XXXV.)

## Strategy XXII

### *Lie*, big-time!

Do it boldfacedly, bodaciously, outrageously, intricately, audaciously, and *flat-out*.

While this Strategy would be reviled by some Anti-Rebel absolutists who decry any level or form of *situational ethics* regardless of any circumstance (such as that under which the great American novelist Mark Twain's memor able boy-hero Huckleberry Finn lied to be able to hide the slave Jim from the slave-catchers per the example cited in Strategy XIV preceding), it's a safe bet that these absolutists would become far less absolute in a twinkling, if they were the ones facing enslavement. Also, it's an even safer bet that they'd be on their knees praying for God or for someone to intercede for them with whatever level of mendacity it might require if they were the ones in danger of getting thrown into the lion's den or into a gas chamber and furnace, to cite two extreme yet *horrifyingly* true historic examples.

The courageous German humanitarian Oskar Schindler did this again sand again, putting his very existence on the line by lying repeatedly to the Nazi authorities about the "technical skills" of the unskilled or underskilled Jews on his famous List in order to save them from the gas chamber and thence from the fiery furnace.

**Strategy XXIII**

**Resort to (gasp!) _blackmail–_ or to the implication of possible blackmail.**

An enrollee in a seminar I taught on Creative Insubordination at the Association of Supervisors of Curriculum Development (ASCD) conference at Boyne Mountain, Michigan in the winter of 1992–and, additionally, one of my graduate students at Oakland University in 1997– came up separately with the following Machiavellian example of this Strategy, which is of highly questionable legality and which I can't in conscience advocate, but which in the spirit of full disclosure I will share with you nonetheless:

> *If you're super ordinate is married and in a professional position where marital infidelity is a conditional factor that could cause his dismissal, and you've got a sultry (and unprincipled dose friend who's a real player and is unflaggingly loyal to you try to fix him up with her.*
>
> *If he succumbs to her wiles, he'll feel compromised by your knowledge of his affair, and he'll be far less likely-ever-to get on your case, whatever your "case" may be.*

Your Insubordinate old author did confessedly and shamefully once arrange for such a situation to obtain in a certain institution of higher education which shall go unnamed. This occurred during an unspecified period many years ago when your Machiavellian old author was a junior administrator there. While I never felt the need to succumb to what would have had to be an obligatory conscienceless ness in order to use this forbidden knowledge to which I was privy for job retention or political advantage, I could have done so most effectively and devastatingly, had I needed to– but it would of course have been terribly wrong.

Nonetheless, the forbidden secret that I, the unnamed lady and this high ranking gentleman mutually and exclusively shared would certainly have proved to be more than sufficient to keep him off my case, had he ever been tempted to get on it.

**Strategy XXIV**

**Get rough *physically*, or *threaten* to.**

I describe the following relevant incident in chapter 47 of A Life on the RUN:

> Being an "old school" educator, when I returned to teach in an inner-city high school on a post-retirement contract in 1999 at the relatively advanced age of 64, I took a recalcitrant and chronically tardy student an insufferably arrogant star fine man on the Detroit Southwestern High School football team named Tom Chastain out into the hall, and got Avery Jackson, Jr., another teacher, to witness what I was about to do. I then removed my glasses and (rather riskily) invited this young football team captain to hit me.
>
> Had he done so, he probably would have put me in the hospital.
>
> Instead, he said, "Don't wanna."
>
> "Well," I responded, "then do you want to do what I tell you to do?"
>
> "Yeh."
>
> "If I tell you to jump three feet in the air, will you do it?"
>
> "Yeh."
>
> "If I tell you to do it three times, will you do it?"
>
> Hesitation, "Yeh."
>
> "Well, to start with, all I want you to do is get to class on time, so go back in there and sit down– and this time, sit in your own seat."
>
> From that day forward, I could do no wrong with that class, nor with that student, who actually began consistently to help me round up some of his tardy classmates, who soon were tardy no longer.

Here's another anecdotal example of this Strategy:

> Seven years after that Southwestern High School incident, I was teaching and administrating in an all-black high school on the other side of town as America's only retired school superintendent who had dared (or perhaps been crazy enough) to return to an inner city high school to teach. In that school, I collared a tall, unruly eleventh-grader and threw him bodily out the classroom door when he refused to leave under his own power. His father came and threatened to sue me for putting choke marks on his neck—marks made by vigorous contact with his collar whereby I had tight hold of him.
>
> Two policemen who happened to be outside the principal's office—friends of mine, one the son of my old elementary school classmate Earl Couch-tried to get me to apologize to the father.
>
> I said to them (within the father's earshot). "Hell no. I won't apologize. I gave his son the kind of instant corrective discipline he should have been giving him years ago. His son should apologize to his classmates for taking his teacher away from teaching in order for me to have to eject him forcibly and then have to go to the office to explain what I did."
>
> The father never did sue me, and the young man's behavior improved markedly after the incident—not just with me in that specific class, but in all of his other classes as well-and his improved behavior had a similarly salutary effect on his grade-point average.
>
> On another occasion in that school— which was reputed to be the toughest in Detroit fin 2007, our kids there stomped an invading outsider to death in the halla student came to my office in the winter of 2008 crutching a note to me from a male science teacher of diminutive stature who was having a somewhat serious discipline problems A student in his class had just threatened to beat him up. I went to the classroom and took the student— Ralph Smallwood cut into the hall, slapped him hard, and inquired. "Is this what you threatened to do to Mr. Lazerieu?" I slapped him again and asked him, "Were you going to do it like this?"
>
> I continued to slap Ralph Smallwood all the way down the hall to my office, where I made him write his science teacher a letter of apology and promise never to threaten him again.

Note: Maybe it needs to be mentioned here that while Strategy XXIV was extremely effective in the examples cited, I definitely don't recommend this Strategy to most teachers, male or female, as a primary strategy. As I said, I was and remain what could definitely be called an "educator of the old school." Educative times and circumstances in our nation's teeming inner cities have altered more than a little– and most assuredly not for the better. The unwisely aggressive style with which I sometimes comported myself as a rookie teacher in the 1950s and again less advisedly and far more unwisely as a grizzled veteran during the first decade of the twenty-first century was in those more innocent 1950s days 80 percent less physically risky and also 90 percent effective in heading off trouble before it had a chance to start up.

Actually, I learned this Strategy and this style from my fighter father rather than from any university course in Education 101, and I confess brought it into play more than once in some venues far removed from academe.

In order to better illustrate how it was that I learned this fully effective but admittedly risky style from my father, please allow me the liberty of digressing a moment to share with you another much earlier example of how I implemented this style of my father's (who in the 1930s had been United Auto Workers president Walter Reuther's smallest and toughest bodyguard at five feet eight and 158 pounds):

> *As a callow 14-year-old who had just begun my second week of study at a predominately black Detroit public high school 62 years ago in the year 1950, I went one morning to the lava-tory, where a bigger student a year or two older than me informed me that I needed to give him a quarter. While I did happen to be in posses son of a single lone quarter. I needed my quarter for lunch money, so I politely asked my new and larger schoolmate why it was that he thought I needed to give him my quarter.*
>
> *"For protection," he told me.*
>
> *I found this to be confusing. "Protection from what?"*
>
> *"Mainly, protection from me, white boy." he answered.*
>
> *"I'm gone kick the living s-out of you if y'all down give me a quarter, and give me it now!"*

> *Finally grasping his meaning and understanding what was about to happen, I put another teaching of my father into prompt practice—namely, get in the first punch, and make it a good one. I accordingly landed a hard left hook squarely between this bullying young shakedown artist's legs, and when he gasped and bent over, I hit him as hard as I could with a right to the jaw that sent him reeling to the floor, where I began to kick the groggy student in the head even harder.*
>
> *"Please stop kicking my head!" pled him.*
>
> *"I will," I promised him, "if you give me a quarter."*

**Strategy XXV**

**Should the circumstances appear to suggest it, confront a threat of violence with a similar counter-threat?**

(Again, I'm being quite serious here.)

> *In a Detroit suburb where I was the superintendent of schools in the Year of our Lord 2009, I brought several hundred Detroit students into my insolvent district to try to balance the budget with the aid of the state's foundation-grant money that followed each student to the district upon his/her enrollment. Hordes of raucous white residents converged on a town hall meeting in the high school auditorium and demanded that the school board fire me for bringing in all these Detroiters. In front of whirring television cameras from Channels 2, 4, and 7, some of the angry citizens actually shouted things like, "We don't want any more black kids walking down our streets and clustering outside and inside our schools. We've already got way more than enough black kids here."*
>
> *A day or two later, one of these angry folks came to my office, pushed past my secretary, and confronted me with these words: "I ought to kick your a–!", whereupon I responded, "Okay, let's go out in the parking lot and you can give it a try."*
>
> *Taken aback more than a little by my response, the jumbo sized gentleman then nevertheless decided that perhaps it would be wiser if he sat down and had a more peaceable and reasonable dialogue concerning the matter, rather than engage in fisticuffs with a scruffy-bearded 73-year-old school superintendent with a broken toe and an uncombed ponytail. After a still-somewhat tempestuous half-hour of discussion, he finally shook my hand, and we peaceably agreed to disagree.*

(A postscript to this incident: I actually did get fired over that issue. The board with one courageous exception– presently buckled to the bigoted mob's demands in the face of threats to egg their cars and break their windows. Curiously, my two immediate predecessors in that superintendence had incidentally been fired as well-and my immediate successor got fired, too. The large suburban county's overweening intermediate (and inter me diary school district ultimately appointed an official from its administrative ranks that this local board couldn't legally fire. The appointee then successfully set about resorting to the same process I had used to balance the budget. At a later point, this astute lady officially became the regular duly board-appointed superintendent, and at this writing I believe that she still sits in that chair-hopefully without having to deal with any further bigotry-engendered tumult.)

## Strategy XXVI

Let's suppose that a) you are an experienced teacher or b) you are an employee of a business enterprise, and you're aware that a) some aspect of the curriculum in your school district or b) some aspect of the business processes in your place of employment are a) obstructing student learning or by obstructing sales, and you so inform your supervisors, but to no avail.

**You might then try, in the case of the school district, to _change this aspect of the curriculum in your classroom to something that WORKS_, or in the case of the business enterprise, _to change how you DO BUSINESS in this regard_.**

> *When as a retired school administrator I returned to teaching in a large inner-city high school English classroom under a special state legislative post-retirement authorization bill affecting that city only, the officious geniuses in the central office had incompetently and unfortunately made a number of adjustments or eliminations to the school district's curriculum that were counter productive to the instructional process.*
>
> *These eliminations included the discontinuation of the very necessary curricula in traditional grammar that the students needed to be taught in order to neutralize their dialectical problems that were interfering with their ability to learn to speak and write the so-called "standard" English of the marketplace.*

> *I therefore began to teach traditional grammar on my own at that school, Detroit Southwestern High School. Meanwhile, I informed my principal, Dr. Betty Hines-whom I had supervised in another school in that city 32 years earlier, and I also informed my department head, Mr. Willie Wooten-that I was teaching the traditional grammar. They both agreed with me that the students needed this instruction.*
>
> *One day a supervisor from downtown named Joyce Moore walked by my classroom and saw my tenth-graders at the blackboard diagramming compound-complex sentences (taking the sentences apart and analyzing their grammatical components and indicating their parts of speech-adverb, adjective, noun, verb. etc.). Horrified, she went straight to the department head and the principal. "Do you know there's a teacher up there teaching diagramming? That's not part of the approved curriculum!"*
>
> *"Yes, we know what he's doing-it's our 'experimental pilot program' in traditional grammar. His students' writing is improving measurably, and he's sharing some of his methods and concepts with the other teachers. As a result, their students' writing is improving, as well."*
>
> *The supervisor dropped the matter.*

## Strategy XXVII

**While bearing in mind the reasoning and admonishment to be found within the advisory content propounded in Strategy XXVI preceding, still do indeed *resist yielding to conform* or urging *others* to conform to archaic, pedantic, and absurd rules of speaking and writing; e.g., to slavishly avoid splitting an infinitive like I just split just because it's the archaic rule not to (as in my usage "to slavishly avoid" in the preceding), or, similarly, to slavishly avoid ending a sentence with a preposition just because it's "the rule."**

> *As Winston Churchill spike ironically on this eminently non-visceral subject, "This is nonsense up with which I will not put!"*

(Strategy XVII naturally applies in other similarly preposterous situations and circumstances, as well.)

## Strategy XXVIII

**Sometimes be intentionally irreverent and even confrontationally rude when this behavior suits the purpose of necessarily embarrassing or de-fanging a bureaucrat or a snob.**

> *When admonished in the presence of other party attendees by an overbearing patrician party hostess for being "in a disgraceful state of drunkenness"-the aforementioned-and-quoted future wartime Prime Minister of Great Britain is said to have loudly and irreverently confessed to this aristocratic lady, in the presence of her other distinguished guests, "Yes, madam, drunk I confess I almost obviously am-and you even more obviously are ugly. But I shall be sober in the morning, and you shall still be ugly."*

## Strategy XXVIII

**Whether or not you feel the imminent need to cathart about anything (as set forth and discussed back in Strategy X), write Creatively Insubordinate poetry in free <u>verse *just for the simple joy of* <u>writing</u> it</u>!**

(Actually, writing in free verse is a Creatively Insubordinate act in and of itself.)

Even though the great Robert Frost-who almost always wrote in rhymed and metered verse- once sourly observed that writing free (unrhymed) verse is "like playing tennis with the net down," it is nevertheless an exhilaratingly liberating experience to be able to write in free-flowing verse about one's thoughts, feelings, agonies, joys, and ambitiously noble intentions to save the world for its children.

So have at it- and indeed, feel free to send me some of your favorite work in care of my publisher (if you would like to).

## Strategy XXIX

**Read your most heartfelt and eloquently Creatively Insubordinate poems silently to yourself before marching forth to confront a visceral trial or challenge, or play your most moving and inspiring music before it.**

> *Many decades ago when I was an international sprinter, and a few years earlier than that when I was an aspiring teen-aged amateur boxer, I would play bagpipe music on my old victrola to get myself up for my bouts or my races. Being a first-generation Scot, this worked quite well for me.*
>
> *I also liked (and still like) to read Kipling's great poem If to myself, or in another more pensive mood, Vachel Lindsay's O Bronco That Would Not Be Broken of Dancing.*

Accordingly and abidingly, commit to the

### Corollary to Strategy XXIX

Try to adhere to the precepts in *The Creative Old Crusader's Credo* as propounded herein and also on page 157 of *What OLD MEN Know*, this loquacious old Sage's perspicaciously sagacious Definitive Dictionary and Almanac of Advice (www.HarmonieParkPress.com. 2011):

> *If I engage in the Creative Crusade, follow me.*
> *If I hesitate in the Creative Crusade, push me.*
> *If I should err in the Creative Crusade, correct me.*
> *If I should falter in the Creative Crusade, uplift me.*
> *If I'm unaware in the Creative Crusade, inform me.*
> *If I should betray the Creative Crusade, kill me.*
> *If I should hunger in the Creative Crusade, feed me.*
> *Should I need aid in the Creative Crusade, assist me.*
> *If I should die in the Creative Crusade, remember me!*
>
> —author unknown
> (adapted from The Window 2 My Soul, the memoirs of my young Creatively Insubordinately crusading comrade, Yusef Shakur [yusefl_shakur@yahoo.com])

Indeed, to express and propound your Creatively Insubordinate cause poetically and *politically* is often a personally and socially rewarding thing to do whether your cause may involve a bloody insurrection or simply an election.

Regarding the *latter*, try <u>this</u> one on for size, which I wrote during the 2012 Republican primaries:

*OBAMA BE PRAISED:*
*AN ELECTORAL LIMERICK*
*Subtitle: What's a NEWT?*
*SUB-Subtitle: What's a TEA-wee?*

*Our resident President*
*Set forth a bright precedent*
*The pre-CEEDING Prez*
*Was too FLAKY to take.*

*The raucous TEA-Partiers*
*Should now back our President*
*With what's left of their FIZZ.*
*Lest they FIZZLE and ACHE!*

*So I say to those TEA-weez, "Yo' MAMA!*
*We all MUST re-elect our Obama*
*He's the man who got rid of Osama!"*

*If the NEWT-ster gets in*
*With his arrogant grin,*
*Our sad nation will suffer BIG TRAUMA!!!*

**Strategy XXX**

**Get in *trouble*.**

Yes, you read this right.

This is actually more an axiom than a *Strategy*– but it is precisely what your ever-Creatively Insubordinate old author advised a group of Detroit Public School principals to do as warranted when I was supervising and evaluating them in 2000-2001. It is also what I advised my Oakland University and Wayne State University classes of urban/suburban educators to do as warranted when I was teaching them in the 1990s and into the twenty-first century. Neither many of my principals nor most of my classes entirely grasped what I was trying to tell them: That with leadership comes the obligatory but often dangerous duty to "get in trouble" for pointing out that "the Emperor has no clothes," when indeed he has none.

Wise Old Educators (WOES-a politically rueful acronym) have long WOE *fully* recognized that although the institution we call "school" is an "agent of society," this august status doesn't absolve it from the responsibility to serve as an agent for the *progressive reconstruction* of that society, as warranted. American democracy's world-wide power and prestige haven't been defined by our economic standing in the world, nor by how many nuclear weapons we've stockpiled. Historically, America's world-wide power and prestige have been defined by our democracy's moral force. The viability of this force is now being threatened from within our own borders. As expressed in the poem *Sonnet for a Safer Sea* to be found near the beginning of this little book, we must find a way to reverse our current devolution from democracy to gridlocked bureaucracy and plutocratic corporatocracy.

And yea, verily, O long-suffering reader, this here Old Poet (and lover of big words) is about to inflict yet another perspicacious poem upon you! As you peruse it, try to imagine it in musical form, because I penned this poem in the form of a brief ballade and sang it over the air on my little Sunday afternoon radio show on WEXL 1340 AM and on my Wednesday evening television show on Channel 33 (Detroit Comcast 20). The poem addresses public-school segregation-just one more of the many issues that the so called "liberal class" which the Pulitzer Prize-winning author Chris Hedges accuses of becoming self-servingly chameleonic in his scathing indictment of false or turncoat former liberals in his 2010 book, Death of the Liberal Class (Nation Books, New York). As you read it, imagine it in musical form:

> <u>De Lay of de "Liberals"</u>:
> *A Deliberately <u>Brief Ballade</u>*
> *Since 'Fifty-four. Brown vs. Board*
> *With sadly meager fuss.*
> *Was bumped beneath the bus.*
> *To postpone desegregation Is cowardly procrastination*
> *Indeed, to delay until even next Saturday*
> *Remains dirty, way low-down immoral <u>maggotry</u>!*

(I whimsically subtitled this poem "A *Deliberately* Brief *Ballade*" instead of "A Deliberately Brief Ballade" for no other reason than that the French ballade sounds fancier than *ballad*, and I made the ballad brief because the backtrack ing "liberals" have given this crucial cause short shrift.)

The word *maggotry* in the last is a *neologism* (Republicans, please check your dictionary again, if you have one). Also, for the information of any of you WASP affiliates of the GOP who may actually still be trying to struggle through this poetry-laden epistle and are haltingly able to decipher and perhaps even appreciate some of its less *nuanced* verse, the first two words in the first line of the title have a double meaning: *delay*, as in *procrastinate* and lay, which means an *ancient ballad*.

And *no*, Republicans!—a lay isn't the tumble in the hay that roving Democrat dogs customarily indulge in with your Elephantine wives. In Medieval English, a lay is a narrative poem intended to be sung. The word evolved from Old French and originated in the Latin.

In addition, the entire first line in the title is couched in bitterly self-mocking and (what is now called) *Ebonics* dialect. My use of the term *self-mocking* would evidently appear at first blush (given my genetic heritage) to be puzzling, but even though I am a first-generation Scottish-American, I have always identified closely with African-Americans—particularly in this specific cause-perhaps even more than some of them identify with and embrace this *democratically essential cause* any longer, themselves!

Another double meaning in the poem can be found in the use of the word *bus*, which has implications for the noble but failed cross-district busing endeavors of the 1970s to achieve racial integration of the public schools. This is one of the egalitarian causes that contemporary so-called "liberals" have entirely abandoned during their decades-long descent into the dismal swamps of economic collusion with corporate crocodiles. In addition to turning its back on school integration, the so-called "liberal class"-even including some black leaders within it has succumbed almost entirely too abject opportunism.

Much of the liberal class has miserably failed to fight and indeed has joined forces with the corporate hijackers and plunderers of our public schools and the exploiters of our public schoolchildren-particularly in urban school districts, as exemplified specifically and starkly in the troubled Detroit Public Schools now into the second decade of this century. The liberal class has cravenly and un-creatively and subordinately failed to defy and root out corporate criminality not only in our schools and colleges, but also in our municipalities, in our legislative and judicial bodies, and even in our churches.

And, out of weakness and fear, it has also betrayed and exiled from its ranks those few truly Creatively Insubordinate liberals like this writer who have remained defiant and in many instances have paid a heavy professional and personal price for that defiance. ("We who put conscience above our careers/Are dying as a breed and are deep reference in *arrears*....")

Finally, for the information of you numerous Repubs who may not be aware of this—or if you *are*, you disapproved of it: The "Brown vs. Board" line in the poem does indeed refer to the landmark 1954 Supreme Court decision that racially separate but "equal" public education is inherently unequal, immoral, un-Constitutional, un-democratic, illegal, and unjust. In that large and wild public high school in Detroit where I returned to administrate and teach between 2003 and 2008, no one would have been able to discern from observing its student population that as an American public school it was required by Federal law to be racially integrated. The students who attended the school were and still are 100 percent African-American, as are the students in most other schools in the city-as well as in hundreds of other urban enclaves all across America. Our nation is indeed undemocratically susceptible to becoming again the "Land of the Fee and the Home of the Slave": Most of America's public schools that house African-American students are illegally segregated separated and overwhelmingly unequal 58 years after that glorious Brown vs. Board of Education decision of 1954.

(For more on the topic of segregation, see my autobiography. A Life on the RUN, and also see "Race and Residential Segregation in Detroit," by john powell and John Telford, and "American Education: Still Separate, Still Unequal," by Arthur Levine, in America's Urban Crisis and the Advent of Color-Blind Politics Education, Incarceration, Segregation, and the Future of U.S. Multiracial Democracy edited by Curtis L. Ivery and Joshua A. Bassett [Lanham; Boulder; New York; Toronto; & Plymouth, UK-Rowman & Littlefield Publishers, Inc., 2011].)

## Strategy XXXI

**Play *dead*.**

This whimsical Strategy comes courtesy of my creatively insubordinate friend and fellow poet Thomas William Kozma. Allow me to cite the following example of this Strategy which Mr. Kozma has kindly submitted for inclusion in this tempestuous tome:

> *Mr. Thomas William Kozma, Creative Insubordinate par excellence, went to a Lens Crafter store one day to pick up a pair of glasses he had ordered. The staff at the store was very busy, and Tom stood waiting for an inordinately long time, along with other increasingly angry and impatient customers who were beginning to complain loudly. Tom had come there directly from work, and he was tired, hungry, and anxious to go home. He had been taking a yoga class where he had learned a position called "the corpse." He creatively and insubordinately decided to lie down right there in the middle of the floor, and he then assumed the supine corpse position.*
>
> *It wasn't long before a clerk came and asked him. "Sir, are you all right?"*
>
> *Tom assured the clerk that he was.*
>
> *A few short minutes later Tom had his glasses and had been hastily hustled out of the store.*

## Strategy XXXII

**Create an artificial scarcity of a desired article or commodity to engender a specific behavior on the part of those who want it.**

You'll recall that this is what Dr. Tresa Zumsteg did with the intentionally scarce shrimp as exemplified in Strategy XIX, when she was a rookie school principal in the Rochester, Michigan Community Schools and she was having trouble getting her staff to arrive at meetings on time. Soon none of them came late, because they all wanted to have a piece of the succulent shrimp. and there wasn't enough to go around.

**Strategy XXXIII**

**To "let off some steam" and also stir up some support for an endangered cause that you espouse, write a Creatively Insubordinately irate letter to a newspaper editor.**

Or else, submit an op-ed column to your local paper fostering your cause.

**Corollary to Strategy XXXIII**

Write still _more_ Creatively Insubordinate poetry!

However, this time, try your hand at the Creatively Insubordinately self-disciplinary act of writing many of the poems in *rhymed* and *metered* verse, and relatively fewer of them in free verse.

I also emphatically suggest that your poems support causes you espouse whether your causes are personal, professional, political, or apolitically humanitarian– and they should often be causes which you are experiencing some frustration in furthering and getting the positive results for them that you desire. Your poems will then become eloquent rallying cries for making your causes come to fruition in the manner in which you wish them to come to fruition.

(And, as I mentioned earlier, you don't have to be professional, published poet to write poetry: You will indeed surprise yourself at how good you get at writing it.)

Your poems thus can also become a means to help you protest passionately and sometimes with bitter irony against some situation or injustice that particularly troubles you. These injustices might include, for example, the paving-over of millions of forest animals' natural habitats that causes them and also causes stray household pets– to fall prey to speeding traffic on the highways, or these injustices could include the callousness of some prison guards in the presence of the human wreckage in their charge, or they could include any of the many other forms of unfairness such as our increasingly classist tax structure or the egregious expense of policing against an innocuous weed such as marijuana. These are all injustices that are selfishly, malevolently and sometimes absurdly enacted by men upon any and all of their fellow sentient beings in our nation and on our planet.

Moreover, your poems can help you to articulate your pertinent personal and/or spiritual philosophy better and with mounting frenzy-whether that philosophy may emerge from a politically conservative or else a Libertarian perspective or from a stridently liberal Democratic one (as obviously does mine).

Here are some example poems that are therefore relevantly and Creatively Insubordinate:

*America. My Love*

*I've laughed and loved and lived in turn*
*With Arab, WASP, and Jew.*
*I've played with, grown with, taught, and learned*
*From Black, Malay, and Sioux.*
*I've reached in love to touch the face*

*Of someone short–and tall:*
*To run and win the human race.*
*We need to love us all!*

*I.Brake for Animals*
*Torn tangles of blood-sticky fur*
*Mark the millionth metamorphosis.*
*This roadside rot,*
*This new carrion,*
*This inconsequential clot*
*Once breathed warm breath on a young girl*
*And licked her face.*

*Bush & Cheney*

*Those knaves need hoisting by their necks.*
*Stretched past the points their necks can flex:*
*While oftentimes the odious*
*Becometh quite malodorous,*
*The sounds of that pair kicking nothing but air*
*Perchance would prove melodious!*

### A Christmas Card c/o the Wayne County Jail

*They found his buggered a-up there a-swingin' fum a sheet.*
*His eyes was bugged-a glassy stare, his feces at his feet.*
*He never got no visit, nor no letter, nor no cheer.*
*He done got sent one Christmas card, but he waren't livin' here.*
*Dig, thass the boguest thang I seen since when one day last week. "*
*The country dude in '17 jump down into the street.*
*The hole he make go eight-inch deep thu reinforced concrete.*
*That got to be the measure of his woody," joked a guard.*
*What a card.*

Note: The incidents in the preceding poem, which I co-authored with Judith Urban when she was working in the jail and I was an official of the Detroit Team for Justice, actually happened-and the guard actually did make that unfeeling remark. (A "woody" is an erection: Ms. Urban felt that the poem would be more impactful if it was written in idiom and dialect.)

### IN A BAGHDAD ALLEY:
### A Transformative Curse
### On the Treasonous Tush
### Of the Traitorous Bush

*May Bush be shipped to Iraq*
*And get transfigured as a fly*
*Adrift above a dying rat*
*Beside a dead one, in July*
*The rats to be fed to a hungry cat*
*That catches and eats the accursed fly*
*For the cat to excrete in the sweltering street,*
*So the fly may emerge in the cat's oozing turd*
*That reeks and secretes in carnivorous heat*
*And then gets gobbled up by a turd-eater bird.*

Note: The *Bush* referenced in the preceding poem is, of course, not the World War II hero George Herbert Walker Bush but rather his catastrophic offspring George W. Also, you won't find the "*turd-eater* bird" in any ornithology book. because the bird doesn't exist. However, had there been such a turd-eating bird called the "*turd-eater* bird," our nation then could only have hoped that the turd-eater bird would have eaten George W. Bush before he had the chance to attack Iraq.

Here follows yet another poem containing a well-deserved curse:

*A Curse upon the Creature*
*Who Killed the Little Girl*

*Detroit, 7/'11: For the late Mariha Smith of Detroit, age 5–*
*a short, raging, rallying cry composed and read over the air*
*on the John Telford Show on Radio Station WQRS FM on Sunday*
*afternoon, July 31, 2011, by the aforementioned horrified*
*radio host–*

*God spare us from atrocities.*
*From monsters and monstrosities*
*Un-rightful and frightful night-crawlers who creep.*
*And slip into bedrooms where innocents sleep.*

Okay that's enough psyche-rattling poetry for at least the next few paragraphs.

Now ruminate on this somewhat unsettling scenario that I lay out for you in the next Strategy:

**Strategy XXXIV**

***Contemplate* and *consider* organizing and mobilizing for a *real revolution* on a national scale.**

This could be a revolt limited, for example, to a movement to *legalize marijuana* in order to save our nation untold billions of dollars in law enforcement and incarceration expenses which could then be diverted to education and preventive health care.

Or– it could be an expanded cause that goes far beyond the legalization of some illegal drugs and metamorphoses to a cyber-revolution and/or a massive series of protests in the streets that ignite a mammoth anti corporate insurrection.

Finally– and far more drastically–it could become a bloody revolution like the historic one that magnificently arose in the Creatively (and insurrectionally) great insubordinates George Washington's and Ben Franklin's America of 1776.

CREATIVE INSUBORDINATION

### *First Corollary to Strategy XXXIV*

Relevantly, write yet more poems with themes featured in, for example, these two that follow.

These next two poems, which I wrote in 2012, express an increasingly anarchic American sentiment that Wall Street, the counter-democratic corporate criminals, and their collusive Demo publicans and Republic rats in Congress and the US. Senate would do well to heed before it's too bloody (and *bloodily*) late:

> <u>Barreling Dogs of War: The Canine Crusade</u>
>
> *For lo these wild years in our Crusade.*
> *We have been akin to the lean wolf*
> *That runs all night and every brutish day*
> *To bring down cloven devils on the hoof.*
> *Now we grizzled, panting/dashing dogs*
> *Exhort you pups: The race is far from won.*
> *To catch and kill the greedy corporate hogs,*
> *Your barreling is barely but begun!*
>
> <u>Comes the Revolution</u>
>
> *It is unfortunately true*
> *That by Two Thousand Twenty-two*
> *Those "One-Percenter" corporate cats*
> *And money-grubbing autocrats*
> *Who make a fateful mockery*
> *Of our once-great democracy*
> *Shall have had a decade's warning*
> *That the Revolution's forming!*
> *All of us should be dissenters –*
> *White and Black, and even Gay!*
> *Dare we "Ninety-nine Percenters"*
> *Grab a Glock or an A-K??*
> *There can be no weak relenters –*
> *Everyone must join the fray!!*
>
> *(Still, some of us are normal men*
> *Who'll rack our rifles now and then*
> *To smoke a joint and have a drink –*
> *And then mayhap and maybe,*

*We'll pause and point and smile and wink
At some attractive lady.)*

I have to warn everyone, though, that not too many swords will be sheathed or pistols holstered, nor will too many of our country's several million privately-owned hunting rifles remain locked away in their cabinets when unemployment insurance runs out and ordinarily law-abiding American men and women can indeed no longer feed their children short of revolution. Are you hearing this, Mssrs. Boehner, Gingrich, Trump, et al.?

**Second Corollary to Strategy XXXIV**

As a last and final resort: organize, mobilize, and carry out the most extreme and ultimate threat within this Strategy.

This of course is something that we can still hope and pray will never become necessary in this country. Yet if all else fails, and we middle-class Americans can indeed no longer feed our children by legal means, this will be the only path that the one-percents will have allowed to remain open for us ninety nine percent to take, and we will then need to be prepared either to prevail or to die trying. Many of the preceding and following Strategies and Corollaries and Sub-Strategies a are naturally to be preferred, and those preferred courses of action should all be followed first and prayerfully.

It is in that preferred and prayed-for spirit of restraint and preventively Strategic, Creatively Insubordinate alternatives that I therefore give you:

**Strategy XXXV**

**Hire a _lawyer_!**

This Strategy bears *repeating, re-amplifying*, and *re-emphasizing*. There exist some unjust and egregious illegalities which one cannot hope to rectify with out professional legal backup.

And don't procrastinate. Some forms of litigation have time restrictions and limitations.

*As also exemplified earlier in Strategy XXI, one of my many post retirement jobs was with the once highly reputable community agency called the Metropolitan Detroit Youth Foundation, whose director hired me in 1992 as his executive deputy. Trusting his word that he had the authority to retain my services, I promptly ordered a set of business cards, hung my plaques and certificates on my office wall, and began to call upon many influential individuals of my close acquaintance to solicit support for the Foundation, which had descended into deep financial difficulty due to major theft on the part of a previous comptroller who subsequently went to jail.*

*Using my contacts and my reputation for honesty and cap ability, I quickly gained many key and lucrative promises of help from these men, and the agency was poised for the comeback trail. Unfortunately for it, I had been on the job less than a month when the organization's unemployed board president decided that he wanted my job. I thereupon was unceremoniously dismissed without a dime of compensation- whereupon I sued, meanwhile making sure that the press knew what was happening to me. The organization unwisely fought the lawsuit, untruthfully claiming that I had never been hired; very soon a judge awarded me a fair sum for my embarrassment and loss of promised employment.*

*The thing that bothered me most about this situation, though, was that I had brought on board one of my former high school athletes who then also was unable to keep his job with the Foundation due to its mendacious administrative corruption and cupidity and resultant insolvency.*

## Strategy XXXVI

### Give of yourself freely and unselfishly.

Yes, give *yourself*! Naturally, I'm not talking here about "giving yourself" to every horny lady who wants to bed you, as some of us wandering old wowsers misguidedly did in our day –I'm talking about truly contributing your time. your heart, and your treasure to help someone less fortunate without seeking ything in return other than the satisfaction of having done something noble. you do this, others will take note and quite likely imitate your deed some time, some way. Many of them may also flock to your egalitarian cause when they note that you are a genuinely loving, giving individual. (And you don't have to be a deeply religious person like Mother Teresa to do this-one can be giving and good, or become giving and good,

# CREATIVE INSUBORDINATION

without being necessarily pious.) Ultra-religious definitely am not-starting in childhood, I've witnessed too much hypocrisy among myriad folks who have included priests and preachers within their ranks who so profess to be.

Once on an impulse I gave my brand new overcoat to a coatless, hungry, homeless black man who was openly pilfering crackers and ketchup in a down town Detroit Coney Island restaurant and was about to be ejected. I also bought him two Coneys.

This empathic Strategy can best be expressed in a poem titled "Salvaging My Soul":

> *I shook the tallest tree:*
> *Pierced every secret door;*
> *Then searched the deepest sea*
> *For what I'd sought on shore.*
>
> *My task was unachieved –*
> *I searched and sought in vain,*
> *Nor gathered why I gave.*
>
> *But now my soul is free:*
> *No more need I explore –*
> *At last it's clear to me:*
> *I gave to be restored.*
>
> *To give is to receive:*
> *To give is to regain;*
> *To give is to be saved.*

Paradoxically, what we genuinely *give*, remains forever *ours*. Indeed, to give is to get. It took your old author a veritable lifetime to learn this more fully, and he's still learning it. Others die without ever learning it or even beginning to learn it.

Winston Churchill once said, "We make a living by what we get, but we make a *life* by what we give." Amen.

# CREATIVE INSUBORDINATION

## Strategy XXXVII

**Always befriend even the lowliest-positioned rank-and-file employees in your organization.**

This is the democratically egalitarian thing to do anyway, and you never can tell when you might need their support or when they might be able to afford you some valuable and needed information that you couldn't otherwise formally garner.

> *When I was a high-ranking young executive of a 17,000-student school district in a suburb several miles west of Detroit in the late 1970s and early 1980s, I had a senior colleague who cautioned me not to fraternize with teachers or custodians, or even with building-level department heads or assistant principals. This elitist chap had overheard an elderly custodian call me John, so he took me aside and advised me not to let a custodian call me by my first name. The old custodian–who had been a commando in the British Army during World War II–spoke with a soft Scottish burr that reminded me of my Scots grandparents. I told my concerned colleague. "This man was fighting the Nazis in North Africa when you were in short pants and your mommy was driving you to nursery school. He can call me anything he wants." I don't know whether the lesson took, but my concerned colleague didn't bring the matter up again.*
>
> *In that same district when my job was endangered due to budget cuts, hundreds of teachers wrote to the board, the super intendent, and the local newspapers demanding that I be retained.*
>
> *Also, in another district where I was an executive administrator later in my career and had consistently confronted some tumultuous political difficulty as a result of my egalitarian initiatives (among other similar initiatives, I was aggressively recruiting and hiring black principals in that 98 percent white district), it was a custodian I had befriended who wrote the most eloquent and effective letter among the many written in my defense–a letter (and letters) that was (were) entirely unsolicited on my part.*

## Strategy XXXVIII

**Give rich people more money.**

*Not*! In 2011, the corporate-collusive Supreme Court ruled that corporations are people. Additionally and egregiously, the political party that has a pachyderm for a symbol actually propounds, fosters, and furthers the notion that the best way to create jobs in this country is to give more money to those who are already filthy rich. Some misguided "leaders" of both parties want super PACs (political action committees) funded by mega-corporations to decide who gets elected. I'm not buying it, nor should any patriotic American. Strategy XXXVIII is the only entirely bogus "Strategy" in this enticing tome but I really couldn't resist including it, if only to lampoon it. Never forget that a great Teacher once walked this earth who wrathfully and righteously drove the moneymen from the temple.

This Strategy instead should rightfully read:

> *"Propound, foster, and further the political philosophies and patriotically egalitarian missions of visionaries like Abraham Lincoln, Eleanor Roosevelt, Harry S. Truman, Robert F. Kennedy, and Martin Luther King, Jr."*

The existence and malevolent influence of super PACS would have been anathema to those five great Americans-and to that One great Teacher. Such plutocratic contrivances are a frighteningly dire endangerment to our cherished and precious American-style democracy.

### Strategy XXXIX

**If you are a former executive, consider doing as I did and return to the trenches in an enterprise you formerly headed in order to gain or regain increased credibility among the rank-and-file in that field, and simultaneously gain some additional relevant credibility with the general public as well.**

In other words, rather than just "talk the talk," "*walk* the *walk*." as it were.

> *When – as partially and incidentally noted in some of the preceding Strategies– I as a retired school executive returned to one inner city alternative high school to counsel and later to two traditional inner-city high school classrooms to actually teach, I gained an astronomical level of credibility in a broad array of environments, including among*

*the endangered staffs and students within those schools. While in urban education such an unlikely return is an undertaking that can frequently be fraught with genuine physical risk (which could indeed demand the real and present services of an actual undertaker), it absolutely will gain that astronomical level of credibility for the rare executive who audaciously dares thus to return-although at this writing, I am unaware of any former public school superintendent (other than myself) who has done this in the volatile arena of urban American secondary education, and I was still doing it in my seventies.*

*And when I did return to an inner-city Detroit high school classroom, I used my fresh credibility as a lever to try to pressure top executives in the Detroit Public Schools to mend their corrupt and classist ways. In the first decade of the twenty-first century, I attended Detroit school board meetings and harangued the board about its decade-long failure to repair my school's swimming pool in order for it to be reopened for my kids to use. I asked them rhetorically whether they thought that my students were indeed public-school kids, and whether they thought that the students in a certain elite and elitist Detroit public high school that I specified to them were indeed public-school kids, and whether they thought that the students in the affluent suburban community of Grosse Point that borders Detroit to the east were indeed public-school kids.*

*When they assured me that they did indeed believe that my students definitely were public-school kids, I asked them again whether they thought that the students in the other school I had mentioned and in the affluent adjoining district had cited were public-school kids, too.*

*When the board assured me that they all definitely were public-school kids, I asked them. "Then do the pools in those other schools definitely work, or are they definitely in disrepair?"*

*"Oh, they definitely do work, you say? Well, the one in my building definitely hasn't worked for nine years. When are you definitely going to have it fixed?"*

Had a public high school pool not worked in suburban Rochester Hills for nine <u>days</u> when was the deputy superintendent there, the Rochester community would have been inclined to call out the National Guard, the Marines, and the Royal Canadian Mounted Police-and I would likely have been fired fast.

At the time when approached the Detroit board on the swimming pool issue, I just happened to be writing and for several years had written my regular newspaper column titled Telford's Telescope in the Detroit-based Michigan Chronicle-the state's largest and oldest African-American-owned newspaper- and I had a half-hour radio show on Sunday afternoons on *News Talk 1200*, a sizable AM station in Detroit that draws considerable urban (and suburban) listeners. Thus, I was also trying to use my column and my show as leverage with the board of education, per the previous Strategies and Corollaries cited here already.

At this writing, I have a column in the Detroit Native SUN-a small community newspaper, and I have a shorter radio show (only fifteen minutes) on Sunday afternoons at 1:45 on WEXL, an AM station that reaches hundreds of thousands of Detroit and suburban listeners. I also have a half-hour television show on Detroit Channel 33 (Comcast 20) on Wednesday evenings at 6:30. On these shows and in that grassroots community newspaper, I continue to try to apply that liberal leverage as best I can in the face of voracious Republican appetites in the Michigan legislature, in other Republican-dominated state legislatures, and in the United States Congress for tearing liberal ideals apart in their teeth and turning back the liberal clock to midnight.

Accordingly, I can attest authoritatively that until June 14, 2012, when the Detroit Board of Education named me interim Superintendent of the Detroit Public Schools by a vote of 7-2, there had remained some board members and still do undoubtedly remain some central office administrators in the Detroit Public Schools who generally wish that I was either dead or else would retire conclusively and then emigrate permanently to the farthest reaches of Outer Mongolia.

And, speaking of *dead*, I give you...

**Strategy XL**

**Threaten actual murder.**

Murder is a *terminal* (literally!) Strategy which of course I'm reluctant to sanction seriously, If for any reason short of military, civil-defensive, or self-defensive action you're even contemplating killing anyone, it would be far better for you (and for the ongoing existence of your contemplated victim) that you cathart instead-á la the Second Corollary to Strategy X-in a poem like this one, written in early 2011:

> The Ancient Blood Code:
> A Tale of Betrayal
> Were my fighter-Scot father
> Still bloody thrashing
> Above the green bloody grass,
> He would forthwith be demanding
> That our Code of Old be fast imposed
> And cause my meandering, philandering.
> Wife-plundering friend across the street
> To become bloody maimed In his penile region pronto,
> Or else be bled bloody bloodless In untimely (yet timely) fashion.
>
> Still,
>
> The ancient, sating sight and sound
> Of dagger drawing traitor blood
> And claymore hacking traitor bone
> Might (in metaphor) but seek
> To stay un-sating and unseen.
> My philandering, plundering, treacherous friend
> Does therefore need indeed to thank
> His bloody luckiest stars that my
> Fierce fighter father's remains remain
> Safely supine and undemanding
> (Albeit perhaps at infinite unrest)
> In bloodless blackness down beneath the grass.
> Un-greening.

Some ancient Scottish patriarchs upheld a Code which their direct male descendants would do better not to follow to the letter in this country and this era. Instead, in accord with the Second Corollary to Strategy X, it would be well for an old first-generation Scots-American such as myself, for example, to pen a poem like the preceding one as catharsis rather than yield to murderous temptation to follow his old family Code and risk squandering away in a musty prison cell the scant time that remains to him beyond the 76 years he's already spent toiling in passage on this planet.

That cautionary point having hopefully been most emphatically and personally driven home to you more impulsive C.I.s who may be unwisely inclined toward murder or mayhem as an optional implementation of some Creatively Insubordinate but overly vengeful act, let me nonetheless share the following true and similarly *personal* incident with you as an example of Strategy XL, in order that you may judge my handling of it:

> When in the year 2000 I took one of my Detroit Southwestern High School students aside and warned him that I was going to call his grandmother if he didn't stop skipping my class, he advised me heatedly that he would slash my tires if I made that call.
>
> Thereupon. I informed him matter-of-factly that if he so much as dared to even touch a single one of my tires, I would have him killed.
>
> He gave me the most incredibly strange look, but he never skipped again, and my tires remained intact. (Also, I never had to call his grandmother.)

This particular young Rebel happened to have an inordinate fondness for messing with teachers' cars in the staff parking lot-particularly with those belonging to teachers he didn't like: He was later caught washing one of their cars with a natural fluid donated directly, with no "middle man." flowing warm and wet–straight from his own personal physiognomy.

This prankish direct donation of yellow, salt-sticky, odiferous bodily fluid could actually be categorized as a surreptitious act of Rogue-style Creative Insubordination, thus classifying its disreputable young perpetrator as a Rogue Rebel rather than simply a Rebel (see the pertinent classification in the up lifting list to follow).

Here is another example of Strategy XL:

> My tall, tough, and characteristically Creatively Insubordinate old friend Walt Chapman had been a street sergeant on hazardous police patrols for many decades in Highland Park, Michigan-an enclave of Detroit, with all of Detroit's raw social problems, and more. As the trail of years in which he had served on this dangerous detail stretched longer and longer behind him, and as he became more and more physically and emotionally scarred by it, he re quested reassignment to a central command post numerous times.

> *To no avail–he was simply far too good on the street. Sgt. Chapman's super ordinates knew they needed to keep him there to make them look good.*
>
> *One night Sgt. Chapman cornered the deputy chief in an otherwise empty lavatory, drew his departmentally-issued .45, pointed the gun straight at his terrified super ordinate's nose, and informed him coolly but intensely that he would "blow his mothering head off" [his actual words if he didn't promise to reassign him at once.*
>
> *Walt got the reassignment he wanted and he got it immediately, with zero repercussions.*

In this situational context, this deputy chief was what I like to classify as a *Non-Rebel*-a blindly unquestioning, sometimes exploitive, often obsequious conformist and a chronically uncreative subordinate.

The Deputy Chief might also be sub-classified as something of an Anti Rebel, with Sgt. Chapman being cast in his perennial role of Rebel (or perhaps radical Rebel-or, more accurately, Rogue Rebel) in that example.

For the purpose of definition and classification in this book. I describe Rebels are those resilient, reason-driven souls whom I also dub Real Righteous Rebels. In effect, they are prototypical Creative Insubordinates-dauntless. egalitarian, free-spirited individuals like you (or like you are potentially) who refuse to sit in an "assigned seat." (Does the eagle flying high in the sky above the mountains have an assigned seat? Does the mustang roaming wild and free on our Western plains have an assigned seat?)

Anti-Rebels are the ideological antithetic of the Creative Insubordinate A benighted ideologue, the Anti-Rebel fears progressive new ideas and adheres steadfastly to the status quo.

In C.I. parlance, there are additional pertinent classifications and definitions of Rebel, Non-Rebel, Anti-Rebel, etc.-and there are other relevant boilerplate descriptors I have devised as well. (I once again refer the reader to What OLD MEN Know - A Definitive Dictionary and Almanac of Advice [www.HarmonieParkPress.com].)

Here follow some terms which the astute student and seriously aspiring practitioner of Creative Insubordination will find beneficial to know and perhaps to apply in interacting with and sizing up associates who fit those classifications or fit some of these additional ones, to wit:

**Conservative**—In the noun form, almost always a Republican (and by definition, an Anti-Rebel).

**Counterfeit Rebel**—A counter-Rebel, an infiltrator in the Creative Insub ordinate's camp. A Counterfeit Rebel is a contra-an insurgent Anti-Rebel in disguise. The Nazi spy Security-the infiltrator of the American POWs, as powerfully portrayed by Peter Graves in the classic film Stalag 17—is a dramatic prototype.

Extremely devious and dangerous, the Counterfeit Rebel must in no way be confused with a *Pseudo*-Rebel (see Pseudo-Rebel, to follow).

**Healthy Irreverence**—A characteristic of all Creative Insubordinates in regard to the earthly "powers-that-be."

It is well to bear ever in mind that quite often, the Emperor does indeed have no clothes.

**Liberal**—In the noun form, almost always an embattled, proud, and proudly *liberal* Democrat or Libertarian who identifies with the causes of racial minorities, and if a non-minority, often actually identifies with the minorities themselves. In our nation's current extremely divisive political climate. a true Liberal is of necessity a Rebel (if he or she is a truly committed Democrat, or a Libertarian).

Let me share with you a personal little poem regarding this classification:

*The Liberal*

*And he was born white*
*His young wife was black.*
*Yet she cursed him and called him*
*The "n" word one night..*
*No curse could be worse.*
*But her curse didn't work,*
*Because him being a Liberal.*
*He liked it, the jerk!*

77

**Most Dogs**—Uncreative subordinates (with apologies to Rin Tin Tin and Lassie).

**Non-Rebel**—This definition is self-evident (see the definition of Un-Creative Subordinate which alphabetically follows).

**Pseudo-Anti-Rebel**—A hybridized, semi-schizophrenic classification that would describe a subject in a truly classic case of clinical psychiatry – which classification will be explored no farther here..

**Pseudo-Rebel**—A Rebel "wanna-be." Pseudo-Rebels will make a big show of breaking some superficial little rule just because it's a rule. Often, Pseudo Rebels will curse a lot-obscenely, loudly, and publicly. The Pseudo-Rebel's only cause is to *conform* to <u>*non-conformity*</u> in a flashy, sometimes swaggeringly bullying manner.

Andrew Dice Clay, the potty-mouthed, faux-macho comic whose star rose high in the late 1980s and early 1990s and plummeted abruptly thereafter. was a perfect prototype of a Pseudo-Rebel. (I once rather uncomfortably shared my name with Clay's on the cover of a Detroit weekly magazine where upon I was the happy cover boy.) A Pseudo-Rebel is what Winston Churchill would call a "sheep in wolf's clothing."

**Radical Rebel**—Often, a redundant appellation. A Radical Rebel in the category's most extreme connotation is a Rebel who doesn't step over the boundary into the Rogue Rebel's renegade territory. (Again, see What OLD MEN Know, and see Rogue Rebel, to follow.)

**"Radical-Chic"** ("Radical-SHEEK")—A hyphenated adjective not to be confused with "Radical Chick"—a female Rebel, or a "radical sheik"—Rudolph Valentino's 1920s film character. (For the benefit of myopic Republicans [a redundancy? the latter two citations are jocularities Republicans, check your dictionary if you have one).)

A behavioral example of "Radical-Chic" is someone-often a staid, nerdy or corporate bureaucrat-who courts famous Rebels or does superficially "daring" things outside the workplace in hopes of being seen governmental as a Rebel, particularly by real Rebels he admires.

A person who exhibits Radical-Chic behavior craves the glamour without A person w the danger of perhaps having to "pay the dues." People like this are often seen in the orbit of prominent athletes-particularly fighters (or of mobsters. from a safer distance). Sometimes the person may even be a celebrity in his own right, but in a less physically risky line of work. An example would be when current teen heartthrob Justin Bieber held boxing star Floyd Mayweather's championship belt and walking behind the fighter in his entourage carried it aloft into the ring before the May weather-Miguel Cotto bout.

Other kinds of Non-Rebel or Pseudo-Rebel can also be "Radical-Chic."

A second good illustration of "Radical-Chic" is the time the late Leonard Bernstein, during his days as the director of the New York Philharmonic Orchestra, gave a trendy, self-consciously liberal cocktail party for the Black Panthers.

**Rebeldom, Under the "Rebel Dome," Rebelhood, Rebelness, Rebelry** – The Creatively Insubordinate world and all it stands for-the state of being a C.I.

**Rebelesque**—Insubordinative in the Creative sense. Like a Rebel-righteously rebellious. Also, Rebelish.

**Rebelesque Synergy**—Also referred to as "Rebel Synergetics," this is the process whereby a mere two or four or a dozen Rebels pool their thinking and energies to generate enough righteously rebellious and Creatively Insub ordinate planning to foment and fuel a thousand revolutions.

**Rebelette** (masculine form: Rebelet)—a) A young distaff Rebel as yet relatively unpracticed in the techniques and strategies of C.I.; or, b) A young woman with Rebelesque potential. (Female affiliates of a male street or motorcycle gang aren't included in this Classification, since they are about as far from being Creatively Insubordinate as one can get, and they are in fact fawningly dependent on male gang members' favor and approval.)

**Rebelize**—To radicalize, render Rebelish.

**Rogue Anti-Rebel**—A bullying, exploitative, totally self-serving Anti-Rebel who stoops to covertly illegal or unfair means to combat Rebels (or who stoops hypocritically to pretend to condemn and to combat Rebels in order to extract political or financial support from Anti-Rebels or Non-Rebels).

Charles Keating, the central figure in the Savings and Loan Scandal during the George H. W. Bush presidency, could probably be cited as an example of a Rogue Anti-Rebel (or maybe he was just a rogue, period).

Lieutenant Colonel Oliver North of the 1990s Iran-Contra contretemps from the Reagan administration is another example. Clergyman Jim Bakker was a particularly lecherous, acquisitive, and thoroughly heinous prototype of the genre. A far more sinister example of a Rogue Anti-Rebel would be a mass murdering monster like Adolf Hitler, Josef Stalin, Cambodia's Pol Pot, Uganda's Idi Amin, or the historic Roman emperors Caligula and Nero.

*Rogue* **Rebel**—A societal renegade, a Rebel gone bad-one whose ends have become primarily selfish or deliberately destructive to the greater society. Often, a Rogue Rebel is also a bully. Benedict Arnold was a Rogue Rebel. Pancho Villa, Aaron Burr, Che Guevara, Frank Sinatra, and Errol Flynn were on the borderline. (And if you Non-Rebel Republicans la redundancy?] don't know who some of these rakehells were. check your encyclopedia [in the unlikely event you have one] to become a fully-affirmed Rebel Historian!)

Confederate Civil War generals and the rank-and-file musket-toting Johnny Rebs of the Confederacy are exempt from this malediction because while their overweening cause was unjust, they didn't see this as injustice in the context of their era-and they were admirably ready to die in defense of their home soil. In fact, over 95 percent of the Confederate Army didn't own slaves.

A more sinister example of Rogue Rebel would be a particularly amoral rock group or rapper, or a hate group, or a gangster, or a presidential assassin. or a suicidal cult leader, or a serial killer.

*Semi*-**Rebel**—An undecided or lukewarm, partial, sometime, borderline, not yet-totally out-of-the-closet, almost rebel. A Semi-Rebel is like a semi-erection. He is "sort of" Creative and/or nearly Insubordinate. With patiently persuasive, stimulative nurturing and coaxing. some Semi-Rebels possess the potential to become upstanding, full-fledged Rebels. Often an unjust deed perpetrated by a member of the power structure upon someone the *Semi*-Rebel is close to can raise the Semi-Rebel to the ful some, tumescent stature of total *Rebelhood*.

**Strategic Intra-Institutional Rebellion (S *I*-IR)**—The calculated application of C.I. by a functionary of an institution in order to modify or reform that institution constructively from inside it.

Throughout a tumultuous career as an educator and a crusader for social justice that spanned well over half a century, your long-suffering author tried his level best-often at great professional and sometimes physical risk-to practice S *I*-IR by, for example, recruiting and hiring minority staff in majority white institutions I directed or superintended, by recruiting minority students in majority white school districts, and by fighting for the rights of my impoverished black students as a teacher, building administrator, and central-office administrator in a large majority-black district chronically "led" by elitist. Self-aggrandizing, venal, inept, corrupt black "leaders." Also, in my early professional years (roughly 1958-69), I was obliged to defend my students and athletes from racist persecution by some white policemen and some assorted other bigots. I also invited the Black Panthers to a political forum at Macomb County College in 1971 against the wishes of the college president when I was an administrator there—and I wasn't being radical-chic.

For more about these events, let me once again encourage you to read A Life on the RUN-Seeking and Safeguarding Social Justice (www.AlifeontheRUN.com). You'll undoubtedly note that I repeatedly slip this advisement (advertisement?) within these purple pages wherever I can, because I really do want you to be familiar with my marvelous memoirs and my other predominantly philosophical book, What OLD MEN Know-A Definitive Dictionary and Almanac of Advice (which incidentally happens to poke a bit of sometimes rather savage albeit richly deserved fun at the members of the political party that uses the elephant as its symbol).

**Strategy**—An essential component within the definition, practice, and application of C.I.

Without Strategy being extant and skillfully and carefully considered, the successful application of Creative Insubordination is nigh unto impossible. It then most likely becomes an unfortunate form of uncreative or semi-Creative Insubordination which may well result in an utter failure or even in a tragic one for its hapless practitioner. Here, the reader needs once again to bear in mind my cautionary and oft-repeated admonition: "Sometimes the Dragon wins."

Anger, timidity, and tentativeness are all inhibitors to the planning and implementation of Creatively Insubordinate Strategy. They either tempt the aspiring C.. to act rashly and impulsively, or else they immobilize him/her.

Let's use the so-called "Sweet Science" of boxing as an example:

> Boxers who when stung sometimes succumb to anger and throw unguarded and wide-open punches carelessly and inaccurately, and they often end up getting resultantly knocked unconscious. The timid and tentative boxer gets kayoed even faster, because he's too mentally and physically immobile at the outset even to plan and mount an attack.

So is it also with aspiring C.I.'s: They mustn't be timid or tentative; however, neither must they ever allow anger to impair their judgment and cause them to strike out rashly and impulsively. They must be tenacious and audacious rather than rash and impulsive.

As John F. Kennedy sagaciously said. "Don't get mad-get even." And as sagaciously say to you in my tumescent tome What OLD MEN Know, "Don't wish ill for your enemy-plan it."

**Subordinate** (subordinate-ate-ate rhymes with "late"); verb transitive—In C.I. parlance, to "subordinate" an antagonist is to render him submissive. When warranted, Creative Insubordinates creatively subordinate their superordinate(s).

**Uncreative subordinate**—A Non-Rebel: someone who leads an unimaginatively conservative, non-reflective life (also called the "unexamined life").

The uncreative subordinate figuratively doesn't have a clue. For example, an uncreative subordinate would consistently and mindlessly vote Republican in a state-wide or national election even if his annual income were far less than six figures.

To illustrate this another way: Were I to have included a definition of "home cooking" in my 2011 book, What OLD MEN Know-A Definitive Dictionary and Almanac of Advice, I would have defined "home cooking" as "where an uncreative subordinate of the Republican persuasion erroneously thinks his wandering wife is when she's actually consorting wildly all the while with some dashing but disreputable (shudder!) Democrat."

An *uncreative subordinate* is the absolute and total *polar opposite* of the C.I.

(You may have some terms and definitions of your own to suggest as additions to the list immediately preceding. You may also have some Strategies in mind to add to the 40 Strategies and their Corollaries and Sub-Corollaries ! have offered you in this torrid treatise. If you do, I would love to learn of them. Please feel free to mail them to me at 8900 E. Jefferson, Suite 1107, Detroit, MI 48214.)

### *To summarize:*

Permit me to emphasize and re-emphasize that in your ultimate determination of your own individual stance toward generating positive change in your professional or personal life-and then you're necessarily taking appropriate Creatively Insubordinate Action (CIA)-which such action could prove to be invariably difficult and may often even be foolhardily dangerous. This can particularly become the case when the action is indeed taken unilaterally rather than collectively.

Again please allow me to emphasize, re-emphasize, and emphasize yet again: Contrary to the familiar fable, sometimes the dastardly DRAGON DOES INDEED WIN!!!

Yes, indeed he does. Then, as I cautioned you way back in the very first Creatively Insubordinate Strategy in this intemperately torrid tome (hope fully without upsetting you excessively), the Dragon does indeed eat the entrails of the then-insufficiently Creative Insubordinate St. George, drink his blood. lick and suck out what's left of it, and gnaw on the martyred, knightly saint's splintered bones. The well-fed Dragon then does indeed pick his teeth with the deceased saint's lance in leisurely fashion-and the fair maiden then does indeed remain un-rescued and has to dwell languidly ever after with a monstrous, scaly, fire-breathing reptile in his drafty castle in Trump Tower-er, I mea Jurassic Park.

And please know that this doesn't just happen metaphorically in some allegory or misty myth from the Dark Ages. It happens in our own very co temporary and real "Dark Ages" in the murky and uneasy dawn of our already chaotic twenty-first century.

In my audacious youth, I was too vacant between the ears (and too wet behind them as well) to be daunted by any of the many fire-breathing Dragons out there. I followed my Creatively Insubordinate vigilante father's St. Georgian example to become a defender of the underdog-to bully bullies and hunt hunters. As already mentioned repeatedly (and boastfully) in this rare and brilliant (rarely brilliant?) book, I also broke several sprinting records, went many medals, and went undefeated at 400 meters representing the United States abroad to sustain our country's international honor and maintain its sprinters' victory string on the track. (That victory string was occasionally snapped when the Americans raced the two great Jamaicans-George Rhoden and Herb McKenley-in the 400.)

Rhoden in 1952 and current 400 record-holders Michael Johnson in 1996 both achieved the two prime goals on the track that were also mine, but which I failed to achieve: winning the 400 in the Olympic Games and breaking the world 400-meter mark. In his 1996 autobiography (incidentally titled Saying the Dragon Harper-Collins, New York, 1996). Johnson wrote, and paraphrase. "After you have stared long enough into the Dragon's eyes, there is nothing left to do but slay the Dragon or die in the Dragon's clutches? For each of us, that challenging 'Dragon' is the thing closest to the center of our lives. is our core, our nemesis, and often our joy." For some, our Dragon is to van squish injustice, or to write the perfect poem, or even simply to reconcile with cherished friends or family after a tragic quarrel or misunderstanding. For others, it is to become the world's greatest violinist, or sculptor, or teacher For Michael Johnson, his Dragon was to run the perfect race—and he did. For me, my Dragon (in my teens and twenties) was his Dragon—to run the perfect race-but I didn't. Even though I outran Olympic champions and broke records and won all those 400 races on the U.S. team in Europe, I didn't get to win the most celebrated of all races and break the most coveted of all records-but I did learn some valuable lessons from my failure to attain my most longed-for of youthful goals. Perhaps the most important lesson learned was how to deal with disappointment. Even Michael Johnson lost races. So did George Rhoden (including one to me). So, indeed, did the immortal Jesse Owens. And even Joe Louis, Muhammad Ali, and the great Sugar Ray Robinson lost fights.

In his autobiography, Michael Johnson gives five "training tips" for dealing with disappointment. First, don't prepare yourself for failure. If you spend time thinking about what could go wrong, it probably will. Second, when you do lose, do it with grace and also with defiance, because you may be remembered by the way you lose even more than by the way you win. Third, write down what went wrong. Make two lists-the things you can control and the things you can't. Then throw the second list away, because the first list is where your work will be. Fourth, don't lose the momentum of your hard training, or your hard study or preparations, or whatever. Look for other places to channel all that energy. Find new Dragons. Learn. Get on with it. Fifth, recognize failure for what it is: a wholly necessary part of the process, the crucible that creates heroes and legends. As that great Olympic champion and world record breaker Michael Johnson wisely counsels, "Ask you what successful person hasn't had to rise from the bottom. Unfortunately, we haven't yet discovered an alternate route to the top."

Nearly half-a-century after going unbeaten in the 400 in Europe representing our country, I set a knightly St. Georgian record that was far more unique than any record I set on a track (and I also love to brag ad infinitum about this exploit, too: I became the only retired school superintendent in US. history to return to a tough inner-city public-school classroom to teach [initially at the wild Detroit Southwestern High School). I was still doing it creatively and perhaps crazily, although not insubordinately at the far wilder Detroit Finney High School at the ill-advised and unlikely age of 72).

In 2009, I set yet another unchallenged American record. This time, it was one which I would have preferred not to claim: I became the fastest-fired school superintendent in U.S. history (after first having become the oldest). My Creatively Insubordinate high crime and misdemeanor was to go on local radio and television stations and invite Detroit kids to enroll in the suburban school district where I was superintending-and enroll they did, by the hundreds.

I did this over the vociferous objections of scores of white resident "Dragons" at a packed town hall meeting to which I was summarily summoned.

There, as recounted already in the example in this little book's Strategy XXV, these raucous reptilian residents cowed the nervous board of education with ingenuously and remarkably racist statements like, "We don't need any more black kids walking down our streets. We've already got too many of them."

Pointing to me, they then added, "And we don't need him, either."

Detroit television Channels 2, 4, and 7 have videotapes of some of that cacophonous April 2009 town hall meeting, as do I. What aren't on video taped or audiotaped record are the threats some of these same residents made to the resident board of education members about how they were going to vandalize their homes and cars if they didn't back down from supporting me-and indeed if they didn't fire me immediately.

I therefore lasted in that Madison District Public Schools Superintendence only a few short months. So, sometimes the Dragon does and the Dragons do indeed win. (And I do heartily hope that you're getting this repetitive message loud and clear.)

*Nonetheless*:

In the final analysis, any Real, Righteous, Risk-taking Rebel (RRRR, actually a redundancy) including my still supra-seditious old self-will continue to initiate appropriate CIA (Creatively Insubordinate Action) as needed and necessary. For any truly Creative Insubordinate, the trailblazing path of CREATIVE INSUB ORDINATION was, is, and will continue to be the one and only route to take until all of our righteous revolutions have been won both personal and professional both local and worldwide.

So, I trust, will all of you Creative Insubordinates or potential C.I.'s out there earnestly endeavor to blaze that path. At some indefinite point in the not-so-distant future, this righteous old racer will be passing the proverbial baton to you righteous young ones.

May you run with it fast and far.

# THE C.I.'s POP-QUIZ PARTY GAMES

*"To play the game, you don't even need to have a party."*
-H. Ross Perot

The time has come now for you to have some great gamey fun quizzing your self on how much I've been able to brainwash you about-whoops! I mean how much you've learned about Rebels and Rebelry from riffling through the scintillating pages of this priceless paean to Rebeldom. You might also Ske to play my Pop-Quiz Games of "un-trivial pursuit" with your friends and family, or at a party, or with a class you're teaching or taking. (I say "un-trivial" because in keeping with the tone of the rest of this Creatively Insubordinate book, these games contain some very serious and some at least semi-serious Items interspersed with others which you'll find to be much more playful than serious.)

If you play the first game with a class, it can be either a group or a whole class activity. I've field-tested it both ways-and both ways, it's deliriously delectable revelry for Rebels. If you go the group route in the class or at a bash, it's even more fun if you have the groups elect a leader in each group. arrive at consensus answers, and then compare them by having the group leaders report them aloud, and then discuss your reasons for assigning which Classification to whom. Players don't necessarily need to have read the book, although having done so does help to give them a better perspective.

You also have my permission, exempt from Copyright ban, to Xerox the pages that contain the Quiz Categories and the List of Rebel/Non-Rebel Items, so you can give each player a copy of the Categories and Items (or scissor the Items into single pieces and put them into a hat to draw out for individual players to address). There are probably a hundred ways you can set all of these games up. Insubordinates do indeed have to be Creative, right?

Note: If you first played Game I before you read some or the entire book you might like to compare the categorizing you did the first time

CREATIVE INSUBORDINATION

you played to the categorizing that you did in this second-time-around session after you've played twice and done more reading. (Remember, too, that there are no hard-and-fast "right" answers for some items in Game I, so actually it's impossible to really "win" or "lose" in it. Opinions can differ even among us brother-and-sister-under-the-skin C.I.'s! That's what gives our rollickingly Rebelesque experiences some of their spice!)

Consider again the following eight Rebel or Non-Rebel "types" in these games and their abbreviations which I have placed in parentheses after them: Anti-Rebel (A-R), Non-Rebel (N-R), Non-Rebel Rat-Fink (N-R R-F), Pseudo-Rebel (PS-R), your righteous old tried-and-true Rebel (R), Rogue Rebel (RR), Rogue Anti-Rebel (R A-R), and Semi-Rebel (S-R).

Now let me run these eight "Types," or Categories by you one more time, with some quickie definitions:

* an ANTI-REBEL (A-R)—often fanatical and a blustering bully—is the ideological opposite and sworn enemy of the Rebel;

* a NON-REBEL (N-R)—a dull, mindlessly unquestioning, ethnocentric, often bigoted, super-conformist capable of spending a significant number of his waking hours sucking halfway up some arrogant bureaucrat boss's descending intestine;

* a NON-REBEL RAT-FINK (N-R R-F)—an utterly unprincipled, snobbish, sneaky. hypocritical, thievishly greedy and even more butt-kissing and bigoted breed of Non-Rebel who-given the opportunity-can also be a bully (but only if his victim is harmless or helpless enough):

* a PSEUDO-REBEL (PS-R)—a self-aggrandizing, tough-talking but gutless poseur who showily conforms to non-conformity and who also is often a bully (but again, only in an absolutely no-risk situation);

* a real REBEL (R)—the classic Creative Insubordinate also sometimes called a Real Righteous Rebel, is either a righteously reason-driven, altruistic, iconoclastic, constantly questioning, dynamic leader or is a dauntless individualist who maximizes his/her talents (or is both):

89

## CREATIVE INSUBORDINATION

*a ROGUE REBEL (RR)—a tough, often murderously dangerous societal renegade-a Rebel either gone bad or one who was bad practically from the day (s)he was born (and yes, little Virginia-if you see some aromatic dude sporting a "Born-To-Be-Bad" tattoo, believe the tattoo):

*a ROGUE ANTI-REBEL (R A-R)—a bullying, exploitative, totally self-serving Anti-Rebel who stoops to covertly illegal or unfair means to combat Rebels (or to hypocritically pretend to combat "those rotten Rebels" in order to get the political or financial support of other Anti-Rebels or of Non-Rebels); and

*a SEMI-REBEL (S-R)—an undecided or lukewarm, sometime, "almost," not yet-totally-out-of-the-closet Rebel.

(You might also like to briefly turn back to the text of the book and review some more complete definitions of the above relevant Rebel Terms that real relevant Rebels need to know.)

In addition, all of you sharp, Creatively Insubordinate game-players will need to add a ninth Category entitled "NONE OF THE ABOVE" (NAX a tenth labeled **"OXYMORON"** (OX)-a contradiction in terms; and an eleventh entitled **REDUNDANCY"** (RED)-needless repetition.

When you get really deep into playing this first intriguing brain-teaser. and there's an item that has completely stymied you, you might find yourself adding yet a twelfth Category which I) **call "DON'T ASK ME, NORBERTI"** (DAMN You don't have to use the name "Norbert." of course you can use Norman or Nunzio or noodnick or nub-nose or numb-nuts or something else begin ning with "n" instead to complete this cutesie little cuss-word acronym. Or you can think of a pithier acronym of your own (particularly if you thspeak with a lithsp).

In addition, feel free to create your own Category(ies).

# CREATIVE INSUBORDINATION

SUGGESTED **INSTRUCTIONS** FOR PLAYING GAME 1, the Rollicking Rebels Pop-Quiz for Classifying "Rebel" - "Non-Rebel" Types:

In the blank after each of the following alphabetically-listed Items, penicillin the proper initials corresponding to one (and, as the mood takes you, maybe occasionally more than one) of the eleven Categories preceding, as you link each listed **Item** to the **Category** where you think it belongs. The items on my generous List consist of persons, behaviors, and traits that match one or more of the eleven Categories. If you're playing this first game with a group, it can be wild whimsy trying to reach group-majority consensus on which Item belongs in which Category. (Good luck-and physically fighting over the answers is against the rules!)

Also, feel free to add some List-Items of your own. And remember-you don't have to go through every single Item on this entire list in one game or one sitting. It can be revisited for enjoyable times again and again.

Game I has no real rules or limits-because I know how you C.I.'s hate rules and limits. Thus, the Game also has neither a beginning nor a true end, except as you yourself decide. Theoretically, it could go on forever and pro-and-con discussion regarding how and why which Category fits which name can provide infinite fun. Also, if you're not familiar with one or more of the individuals listed, you might want to research them on the Internet (or else just Creatively Insubordinately skip them).

My own sample answers to all of these Items in the first Game, which are purely my opinion, are at the end of the segment. (No fair peeking before you play! Hint-you'll probably not be surprised to find "R" -"Rebel"--to be the most frequent of my personal answers, but watch out for oxymorons or redundancies I've planted in there, because some of them are Rebelishly sneaky.) To get you started in the first game, I'll give you my versions of what think the answers to the first three items should be. All that being said, light the sacred C.I. torch, and let the Games begin!

# GAME I:
## CLASSIFYING "REBEL" - "NON-REBEL" TYPES

### A
Abolitionist, circa 1862_____R_____ (Rebel)
accepts all teachings as gospel on faith alone_____N-R_____ (Non-Rebel)
accepts no "absolutes"_____R_____ (Rebel)
actively supports the status quo A-R (Anti-Rebel)_____
Activist_____
Al Muhammad_____
always agrees with the boss_____
Amin, Idi_____
any female Homo Sapiens over the age of sixteen who allows herself to be called "Bambi," "Muffy," or something cutely similar_____ any principal, superintendent of schools, or board-of-education member who is intimidated by a teacher-empowerment model or by the very notion of empowering teachers_____
a proponent of the "What-would-the-neighbors-say/think?" philosophical school_____
Arkin, Alan_____
Ashcroft, John_____
Assange, Julian_____
associates closely and comfortably only with safe and well-credentialed Non-Rebels_____
author of this book (be honest, please-or at least, be kind)_____
autocrat_____

### B
Bakker, Rev. Jim_____
Barker, Ma_____
Barr, Roseanne_____
Barrow, Clyde_____
Batman (as portrayed in the movies by Michael Keaton)_____

CREATIVE INSUBORDINATION

Batman (as portrayed in the TV series by Adam West)_____
bears constantly in mind that the Chinese word for "crisis" is characterized by combining two symbols-one representing "danger," and the other "opportunity"_____
Beauvoir. Simone de_____
believes that what can be conceived can be achieved_____
Bernstein, Leonard_____
Bieber, Justin_____
Bobbitt, Lorena (remember her? She "bobbed" her husband's private part)_____
Bono, Chaz_____
bootlegger, circa 1920's_____
bootlicker, circa any era_____
Brando, Marlon_____
Brown, John_____
Bruce, Lennie_____
Buchanan, Pat_____
bureaucrat who sells his goods and skills to the highest bidder regardless of principle_____
Bush. George H. W._____
Bush, George W._____

# C

calculatedly and Creatively Insubordinate when necessary_____
can't figure out why his/her kids turned out to be such wild C.I.'s_____
Casanova, Giacomo Jacapo,_____
Castro, Fidel_____
cat_____
cat-hater_____
cat-lover_____
censor_____
champion of positive change_____
Chaplin, Sir Charles ("Charlie")_____
characterized by all three of the essential components of "heart"-courage, perseverence, and caring_____
Chavez, Cesar_____

93

Chavez, Hugo_____
Cheney, Dick_____
Cher_____
Churchill, Lord Winston_____
circumstances don't create him-they reveal him_____
Clay, Andrew Dice_____
Clinton, Hillary_____
Clinton, William Jefferson (Bill)_____
Cochise_____
Cohen, Sasha Baron_____
Columbo (TV detective)_____
Columbus, Christopher_____
conforming Creative Insubordinate_____
confronts bigotry head-on and immediately_____
consultant_____
could characteristically embrace over fifty controversial causes in this that need to be immediately addressed_____
crusading bureaucrat_____
crusading Non-Rebel_____
"cultural relativist"_____
cummings, e. e._____
C.YA. ("Cover Your_ss") is practically their religion when it comes to watching out for their own sses-but they worry little if at all about anyone else's_____
Cyrano de Bergerac_____

# D

dauntless individualist who celebrates life in resiliently innovative ways_____
David (Biblical shepherd boy)_____
Dean, James_____
DeGeneres, Ellen_____
Dessalines, Jean-Jacques_____
Dickenson, Emily_____
Dillinger, John_____
dispassionate dull_____

"disruptive element"_____
"disruptive elephant"_____
divergent thinker_____
Don Quixote_____
Dongfang, Han_____
Dr. Seuss_____
dresses as casually (or flamboyantly) in the workplace as he can, in order to impress others with his "Rebelness"_____
Duke, David_____
Duliere, Warren_____
Dumas, Alexandre_____
Duvalier, "Papa Doc"_____
Dyer, Dr. Wayne Walter_____

# E
Earhart, Amelia_____
easily-led_____
Eastwood, Clint_____
Einstein, Albert endangered species_____
exploits the exploiters_____

# F
farts openly and noisily_____
farts surreptitiously_____
fears any form of innovative or divergent thought_____
feels an automatic aversion to anything the least bit dangerous or "not nice"_____
feels an overwhelming compulsion to determine his/her ultimate destiny_____
Feiger, Geoffrey_____
Fields, W. C. flatterer_____
Flynn, Errol_____
follower_____
Frank, Barney_____
Franklin, Benjamin_____

frequent demonstrator of the Rebel's Easy Technique for Losing Weight Without Even Getting Out of Bed (R.E.T.L.W.W.E.G.O.B.) to other people's spouses_____
Friedan, Betty_____
Frost, Robert_____

# G

gadfly_____
gambler_____
Gandhi, Mohandas Karamchand (the Mahatma)_____
given a choice of fostering the long-term common good or personally gaining from short-term expedience, invariably chooses the latter course_____
goes "by the book" (unless it's this book)-particularly if he thinks anyone is watching_____
Goliath (Biblical giant)_____
Gore, Al_____
Gotti, John_____
governmental, corporate, and educational leaders who fail to ask hard moral questions from deep down inside their guts about the institutions they lead, in order to find the answers that will give our children a fairer future_____
Graziano, Rocky_____
great, courageous, and visionary educators-the ones who design cooperative educational models to transform traditional processes and relationships rather than perpetuate patterns that stratify us by rank and race and class and age and appearance and gender_____
groupie (of any kind)_____
guerilla_____
Guevara, Che_____

# H

Harlan, John Marshall_____
Harris, Sydney_____
has been known to don the garb of the enemy as "camouflage"_____

hates following any kind of rule-and gleefully subverts ridiculous ones_____
or mobilizes to change them- (Note: this book's original working title was The Rebel's Rulebook until one of your author's intrepid friends pointed out to him that the concept of a Rebel following rules was oxymoronic.)_____
healthily irreverent_____
Heep, Uriah_____
Hefner, Hugh_____
Heller, Joseph_____
Hentoff, Nat_____
Heston, Charlton_____
hides behind committees to avoid making decisions on sticky issues_____
higher-level bureaucrat who orders a lower-level bureaucrat not to let a custodian call him by his first name or have a drink with him-even though this custodian had been fighting in the British Commandos during the Second World War while the higher-level bureaucrat's mommy and daddy were sending him off to Montessori Pre-School every day in short pants (Bonus item: what the lower-level bureaucrat is if he follows the higher-level bureaucrat's order_____
Hill, Anita_____
(his vision of cultures other than his is distorted by the ethnocentric "prism" through which he views his own culture)_____
Hitler, Adolph_____
Hoffa, Jimmy (the elder)._____
Hoffa, Jimmy (the younger)_____
honest lawyer_____
Hoover, J. Edgar_____
humanist_____
Humanist_____
hypocrite_____

# I
iconoclast_____
illegal law_____

independent lobbyist_____

Integrationist_____

is wary lest his vision of other cultures be distorted by the ethnocentric "prism" through which he knows he naturally tends to view his own culture_____

# J

jackal"_____

Jackson, Gen. Thomas J. "Stonewall"_____

James, Jesse_____

Jesus Christ_____

Johnson, Jack_____

Jong. Erica_____

jumps on any bandwagon that is gaining obviously superior speed_____

# K

Keating, Jr., Charles_____

Keller, Helen_____

Kennedy, John F._____

Kennedy, Robert F._____

Kerouac. Jack_____

Kevorkian, Dr. Jack Kilpatrick,_____

Kwame, former Detroit mayor_____

King, Jr., the Rev. Martin Luther,_____

King George III of England, circa 1776_____

King Louis XVI of France, circa 1789_____

Knight, Bobby_____

knows that if you're killed fighting for your cause, you didn't really die_____

knows that indecisive leaders must be immediately replaced in times of crisis_____

knows that "the Emperor has no clothes," and says so_____

knows that "the Emperor has no clothes," but is afraid to say so_____

Koresh, David_____

# L

Laden, Osama bin_____
Lawrence Welk fan_____
leader who is altruistic, idealistic, indomitable, liberative, and trans figurative_____
leads an abjectly unreflective life (also called the "unexamined life")_____
least likely Type, statistically, to provide bed partner with complete and consistent orgasm (or any kind of orgasm at all, ever, in life)_____
LeDuff, Charlie (Investigative reporter. Detroit Fox TV)_____
Limbaugh, Rush_____
Lindbergh, Charles_____
lobbyist_____
"lone wolf"_____
lover (active and physical) of other people's spouses_____
lover, more likely than not, of gypsy violin music_____
lover of all of life's peaks and precipices_____
loves to mind other people's business_____
Luther, Martin_____
lying lawyer_____
lying politician_____

# M

Madonna_____
many women who keep their own names when they marry_____
Marshall. Thurgood_____
Marx, Groucho_____
Marx, Karl_____
masters the use of "Bureaucratese" and "Educationese"-and then uses this expertise to obfuscate, pontificate, prevaricate, and steal_____
masters the use of "bureaucratese" and "educationese"-but only for purely and beautifully subversive reasons McCarthy, Sen. Joseph P._____
member of lynch mob_____
mildly malcontented democrat with a small "d" who'd still rather go fishing than fight for freedom._____
Miss America_____

CREATIVE INSUBORDINATION

Miss Nude America_____
most dogs_____
most likely be cruel to animals_____
most paranoid of all the "types"_____
Murphy, Eddie_____
Mussolini. Benito_____
mustang running wild on the plains (does he have an "assigned
    seat"?)_____

# N
Nader, Ralph_____
Napoleon_____
narrow-minded_____
natural-born risk-taker_____
Neruda, Pablo_____
never a part of a herd or flock (or mob)_____
never stays in any kind of irretrievable "marriage"_____
never uses vulgar slang in writings or utterances_____
never would submit to a bully_____
Nixon, Richard M._____
non-conforming Non-Rebel_____
non-conforming Rebel_____
Non-Rebel bureaucrat_____
Non-Rebel Non-Rebel_____
North, U.S.M.C. Lt. Col. (ret.) Oliver_____

# O
Obama, Barack H._____
more idealistic than pragmatic_____
one of his greatest pleasures is doing what people say he can't or
    shouldn't_____
only real hobbies often are either noble-cause-related or romance-related
    and often exclusively the former_____
opponent of explicit anti-AIDS education in the schools_____
Ozzie and Harriet_____

# P

Palin, Sarah_____
Parker, Bonnie_____
Parker, Dorothy_____
passionately romances a noble cause, or mission_____
passively accepts the status quo_____
patriotic lobbyist_____
Patton, Gen. George S._____
Paul, Rand_____
Paul, Ron_____
Paul, Rue_____
Penn, Sean_____
perennially ready to go forth and discover new worlds_____
Perkins, Huel, Fox TV2 anchor, Metro Detroit_____
Perry, Rick_____
personal survival at any cost is paramount goal_____
personal survival to fight another day is ordinarily a strategic goal, but_____
never at the expense of a cause or of the well-being of an ally or friend_____
Picasso, Pablo_____
picks nose covertly_____
picks nose overtly_____
"pillar of the community"_____
pirate_____
Pitt, Brad_____
platitudinous_____
Platypus_____
plunges passionately into any and all of life's adventures head-first-with an open heart that anyone can read like a book_____
Poseur_____
possesses sufficient self-esteem to be unthreatened able to foster it in others_____
Powell, Colin_____
Prohibitionist_____
promotes the distribution of condoms in schools_____

proponent of "trickle-down" economics_____
proponent of an unjust law_____

## Q
Quayle, Dan_____
Queen Guinevere_____
Queen Marie Antoinette_____

## R
"radical-chic"_____
radical Non-Rebel radical Rebel_____
Rand, Ayn_____
ready to follow any rule set down for him or for anyone-regardless of whether some convoluted lunacy or even a typographical error has rendered it ridiculous_____
Reagan, Ronald_____
recognizes that it sometimes takes more courage not to fight_____
recognizes that no job is worth the price of compromised integrity_____
recognizes that the power and magnetism of one's mission and one's message—and what and who one is inside-bear far more weight than one's clothes or hair style_____
recognizes that there are times when to dare is the highest and noblest wisdom_____
regards hypocrisy as the human mind's most vicious mechanism_____
religious fundamentalist whose dogma is utterly incompatible with democracy in that he insists upon his prerogatives as first principles and also insists upon imposing those principles on everybody else_____
relishes the role of underdog_____
reluctant to follow anyone else's rules_____
reluctant to follow rules, period_____
renegade_____
repeatedly and pompously uses the neologized Educationese verb "incentivize"_____
restless soul who would rather go to Hell if it were lively than dreamily drift in Heaven_____

retains a reserve of spiritual strength that enables him first to survive, to thrive, and ultimately to prevail when under attack by seemingly superior forces_____
righteous in the real and true sense of the word-not self-righteous_____
Rivera, Diego_____
Rob Roy_____
Robertson, Pat_____
Robeson, Paul_____
Robespierre, Maximilian Robin Hood_____
Rogers, Will_____
Romney, George_____
Romney, Mitt_____
Roosevelt, Eleanor_____

# S

Sakharov, Andrei_____
Sandusky, Jerry (convicted child molester)_____
Sartre, Jean-Paul_____
Schindler, Oskar_____
seeks out and associates with creative and imaginative people of any background or lifestyle_____
seeks to join the "right" sorority or fraternity_____
segregationist_____
self-righteous_____
self-serving lobbyist_____
Shakespeare, in his timeless play Julius Caesar, calls them "petty men who peep about to find themselves dishonorable graves"_____
"sheep in sheep's clothing"_____
"sheep in wolf's clothing"_____
Siegel. Benjamin ("Bugsy")_____
Silver, Long Dong Silver, Long John_____
Sinclair, Upton_____
Socrates_____
somehow changes the world for the better_____
someone apt to have a dog named "Checkers"_____
someone apt to have a dog named "Cochise"_____

someone apt to have a dog named "Trixie"_____
someone not of Native-American descent who constantly, extensively, and ostentatiously sports Native-American attire: or someone from the northeastern part of the country who obsessively dresses "western"_____
someone quite likely to have a cat named "Dog"_____
Someone the author of this book needs to have on the scene so he can have somebody to poke fun at once in a while_____
someone who is open to marriage or an overt liaison with a vibrant opposite sex (or same-sex) person of any race, class, or religion- and doesn't care who knows about it (and someone who would sanction such a marriage or liaison if it involved his/her own son or daughter)_____
someone who would gladly go to bed with an attractive opposite-sex (or same of sex) person of another race, class, or religion-but only if nobody else_____
knew about it_____
Spartacus_____
Spielberg, Steven_____
Springer, Jerry_____
Steinbeck, John_____
Supreme Court Justice who thinks corporations are people_____
Sutton, Willie "the Actor"_____
Swaggart, Rev. Jimmy_____
Swift, Jonathan_____

# T
Taylor, Elizabeth_____
"Teflon" individual marvelously adept at avoiding or shifting blame_____
tends to make most "pillars of the community" very uneasy_____
tends toward untidiness_____
the best lover, according to this book (and reliable research?)_____
the eagle in the sky (does he have an assigned seat?)_____
the "Joker" as portrayed on film by Jack Nicholson_____
the unique individual psyche's last living romanticist_____

thinks women's primary reason for existence on this earth is to please men_____
Thomas, Clarence_____
Thoreau, H. D._____
timid_____
treats beggars and kings just the same_____
tries, invariably, to vote with the majority_____
"tries not to think about it" as a psychologically repressive mechanism for coping with societal ills (and as the ultimate safe-sex practice)_____
Truman, Harry S._____
truthful politician_____
Twain, Mark_____

# U
Unanue, Manuel de Dios_____
uncontrollable_____
"underground," á la the free French Resistance, circa 1940's_____
uses shock words to blast the barnacles off people and energize them to take positive reformative action_____

# V
values the vigor of slang and recognizes that it is created in a spirit of exuberant defiance_____
very tidy_____
volunteers to picket in front of a slum landlord's home at any time except on his bowling night or when an NFL, NBA, or NHL game is on TV, or if any other piddling exigency he regards as a higher priority should present itself at the last minute_____

# W
Wallace, Sir William_____
Wallenberg, Raoul_____
Washington, George_____
Wayne, John_____
Wayne Newton fan_____
West, Cornel_____

CREATIVE INSUBORDINATION

West, Mae_____
Whoopi Goldberg (the one and only Whoopster)_____
Wisian (see What OLD MEN Know. Harmonie Park Press. p. 264)_____
wolf in sheep's clothing_____
wolf in wolf's clothing_____
woman (now divorced) who showed her nervous new lovers over twenty trophies-featuring figures in various exotic sexual positions-which she had won in public sex contests in partnership with her ex_____
(This really happened-and not on The Jerry Springer Show)
   Woodward & Bernstein would go to great lengths to try to prevent impressionable_____
would make a good, reliable, rank-and-file Nazi_____
would personally subdivide the people, the area and profit from the process without a modicum of regret or guilt (see next item)_____
would stand by and let the Redwood_____
subdivision built with the butchered wood_____
Forest be cut down and replaced by a_____
Wright, Frank Lloyd_____
Wylie, Philip_____

# X

X, Malcolm_____
xenophobe_____
Xerxes_____

# Y

Yevtushenko, Yevgeny Aleksandrovich_____
you_____
your best friend_____
your favorite public figure, past or present_____(name and category)_____
your least-favorite public figure_____(name and category)_____
your parents_____
your playmates who are playing this game with you_____

## CREATIVE INSUBORDINATION

your "significant other"_____
your worst enemy, if you have one_____

## Z
Zapata, Emiliano_____
Zimmerman, George_____

        Have fun!!!

# GAME II:
## YOUR OWN PERSONAL "CREATIVE INSUBORDINATE" SCALE (PCIS)

Answer "agree" or "disagree" to the following ten statements:

1. You dress to suit yourself.
2. You're never the "passive partner" in a relationship.
3. You think Rush Limbaugh, Newt Gingrich, and George W. Bush are buffoons.
4. You think Bill Clinton was a political waffler.
5. You're sexually "straight" but you still openly defend gay rights.
6. You would date a member of another race.
7. You would marry a member of another race.
8. You would find it acceptable if your son or daughter married a member of another race.
9. You prefer blank verse to metered poetry.
10. You'd risk jail or death to further a righteous but controversial cause.

If you agree with none of the above, you're a totally uncreative subordinate. One to three "agrees" make you a semi, not-yet-totally-out-of-the-closet NYTOOTC-colloquially, "not yet, tootsie!") Creative Insubordinate. Four to six "agrees" credential you as a full-fledged, card-carrying C.I. Seven to eight make you a sublime C.I. extraordinaire; and nine to ten render you either a radical revolutionary or a madman, you raving Rebel rascal!

Author's answers (opinion) to GAME 1-Classifying "Rebel" and "Non-Rebel" Types:

# A

Abolitionist, circa 1862-R (Rebel); accepts all teachings as gospel-N-R (Non Rebel); accepts no "absolutes"-R (Rebel): actively supports the status quo A-R (Anti-Rebel); Activist-R: Ali-R: always agrees with the boss-N-R: Amin-R A-R (Rogue Anti-Rebel); any female Homo Sapiens over the age of sixteen who allows herself to be called "Bambi." "Muffy," etc.-either an N-R, an immature and impressionably bubble-brained girl, or an exotic dancer: official intimidated by teacher-empowerment-A-R: a proponent of "What would the neighbors say/think?"-N-R; Arkin-R; Ashcroft-RA-R (The West's version of a Taliban zealot [makes one nostalgic for Janet Reno]): Assange-R: associates only with N-R's-N-R: author of this book-R: autocrat-A-R

# B

Bakker-RA-R: Barker-RA-R; Barr-R; Barrow-RR: Batman (Adam West) bumpkinesque N-R; Batman (Michael Keaton)-definite R: bears in mind that crisis presents both danger and opportunity-R: Beauvoir-R: believes that what can be conceived can be achieved-R: Bernstein-PS-R: Bieber-PS-R: Bobbitt-R (men will probably say RR [Rogue Rebell]): Bonnie & Clyde-RR's:

Bono-R: bootlegger-RR; bootlicker-N-R: Brando-R; Brown-R; Bruce R: Buchanan-mealy-mouthed A-R: bureaucrat who sells out-N-RR-F (Non Rebel Rat-Fink); Bush, G. H. W.-A-R; Bush, G. W.-R A-R

# C

calculatedly insubordinate-R; can't figure out why his/her kids turned out to be C.I.'s-R: Casanova-RR: Castro-RR; cat-R; cat-hater-A-R; cat-lover R:

censor-A-R: champion of change-R: Chaplin-R: characterized by all three components of "heart"-R; Chavez, C.-R: Chavez, H.-R; Cheney-RA-R; Cher-PS-R (Pseudo-Rebel), with some Rebel potential; Churchill-R; circum stances reveal him-R: Clay-PS-R; Clinton, H.-R; Clinton, W. J.-S-R (Semi Rebel) with indications of Rebel potential, since the First Pet, Socks, was a cat -the premier Rebel pet (however, it must be noted that as irrefutable a source as the legendary Dan Rather, after interviewing Clinton on 48 Hours, pronounced him as "relaxed as a pound of liver"-and not too many real Rebels are ever that laid-back, but we love him anyway); Cochise-R; Cohen-R: Columbo-R; Columbus-R; conforming Rebel-OX (oxymoron); confronts bigotry head-on and immediately-R; consultant-N-R (or retired R); could characteristically embrace 50-plus needy causes-R; crusading bureaucrat OX: crusading Non-Rebel-OX:"cultural relativist"-N-R: cummings-R: "C.YA" is practically their religion-N-R's: Cyrano-R

# D

dauntless individualist-R; David-R; Dean-R; DeGeneres-R; Dessalines R. Dickenson-R: Dillinger-RR: dispassionate and dull-N-R: "disruptive element"-R: "disruptive elephant"-R; divergent thinker-R; Don Quixote R: Dongfang-R; Dr. Seuss-R; dresses to impress others with his "Rebelness" PS-R; Duke-R A-R; Duliere-R: Dumas-R; Duvalier-A-R; Dyer-R

# E

Earhart-R; easily-led-N-R; Eastwood-R; Einstein-R; endangered species -R: exploits the exploiters-R

# F

farts openly and noisily-PS-R: farts surreptitiously-N-R; fears divergent thought-A-R; feels aversion to anything dangerous or "not nice"-N-R; feels compulsion to determine ultimate destiny-R; Feiger-R: Fields-R:

flatterer N-R: Flynn-R: follower-N-R; Frank-R: Franklin-R; frequent demonstrator of easy weight losing technique with and to other people's spouses-RR: Friedan-R: Frost-R

# G

gadfly-R: gambler-R: Gandhi-R; given choice of fostering common good or gaining from short-term expedience, chooses latter course-N-R R-F; goes "by the book"-N-R; Goliath-A-R; Gore-R; Gotti-RR; governmental, corporate, and educational leaders who fail to ask hard moral questions about institutions they lead-N-R's: Graziano-RR: great and visionary educators-R's; groupie -NA (none of the above-fanatically neurotic or even psychotic); guerilla-R; Guevara-R

# H

Harlan-R: Harris-R; has been known to don garb of enemy-R; hates following rules-R; healthily irreverent-R; Heep-R A-R; Hefner-R: Heller-R: Hentoff-R; Heston-A-R; hides behind committees-N-R; higher-level bureau crat who orders subordinate not to socialize w/custodian-N-R; lower-level bureaucrat if he follows the order-N-R; Hill-R; his vision of cultures, etc.— N-R or A-R; Hitler-perhaps actually NA-a monster); Hoffa (the elder) probably a RR; Hoffa (the younger)-A-R; honest lawyer-OX: Hoover-R: humanist-R (usually); Humanist-R; hypocrite-N-R R-F, R A-R, or PS-R

# I

iconoclast-R: illegal law-OX: independent lobbyist-OX: Integrationist R: is wary lest his vision of other cultures be distorted by the "prism" of his ownculture-R

# J

"jackal"-N-R or N-R R-F: Jackson-R: James-RR: Jesus-R: Johnson-R Jong-R: jumps on bandwagon-N-R

# K

Keating-RA-R; Keller-R: JFK-R: RFK-R: Kerouac, Jack-R: Kevorkian-R; Kilpatrick-RR: King, Martin Luther, Jr.-R; King George III-A-R: King Louis XVI-A-R; Knight-RR; knows if you're killed for your cause, you didn't die R; knows indecisive leaders must be replaced-R; knows that "the emperor has no clothes"-R; knows that, etc.-N-R; Koresh-NA (monstrous fanatic)

# L

Laden-unclassifiable: beyond the pale; Lawrence Welk fan-often an N-R: leader who is altruistic, etc.-R (usually); leads unreflective life-N-R; least likely Type to provide feminine partner with consistent (or any) orgasm-N-R Republican (a probable redundancy); LeDuff-R; Limbaugh-A-R; Lindbergh R or A-R (a tough one); lobbyist-N-R R-F; "lone wolf"-R; lover of others' spouses-R (too often); lover of gypsy violin-R; lover of all life's peaks and precipices-R: loves to mind other people's business-A-R; Luther-R; lying lawyer-RED (redundancy); lying politician-RED

# M

Madonna-R; many females who keep own names when they marry-R's: Marshall-R; Marx, Groucho-R; Marx, Karl-R; uses mastery of "Bureaucratese" and "Educationese" to obfuscate, pontificate, prevaricate, and steal-N-R R-F: masters "bureaucratese" and "educationese" for purely and beautifully subversive reasons-R; McCarthy-RA-R; member of lynch mob-N-R R-F or RA-R; mildly malcontented democrat who'd rather go fishing than fight for freedom-5-R (Semi-Rebel); Miss America-N-R (an absolute incarnate anti thesis of the concept "Creative Insubordinate," Miss America is always glad to have been crowned, because now she intends, by gosh, to get out there and make the world a better place in her own little way): Miss Nude America Rmost dogs-NR's; most likely to be cruel to animals-N-R R-F: most paranoid of all the "types"-A-R: Murphy-R: Mussolini-R A-R: mustang-R

# N

Nader-R: Napoleon-A-R; narrow-minded-A-R: natural-born risk-taker-R: Neruda-R: never part of a herd, etc.-R: never stays in irretrievable "marriage"-R; never uses vulgar slang-N-R; never would submit to bullying -R: Nixon-R A-R: non-conforming Non-Rebel-OX: non-conforming Rebel-RED: Non-Rebel bureaucrat-RED; Non-Rebel Non-Rebel-RED; North-RA-R

# O

Obama-R: often more idealistic than pragmatic-R; one of his greatest pleasures is doing what people say he can't or shouldn't-R; only hobbies are often either cause-related or romance-related-R: opponent of anti AIDS education in schools-A-R: Ozzie and Harriet-N-R's

# P

Palin-R: Parker, Bonny-RR; Parker, Dorothy-R: passionately romances cause. or mission-R: passively accepts status quo-N-R: patriotic lobbyist-OX: Patton-R; Paul, Rand-A-R; Paul, Ron-R: Paul, Rue-R: Penn-R: perennially ready to go forth and discover new worlds-R: Perkins-R: Perry-A-R: personal another day is goal, but never at the expense of a cause or the well-being of survival at any cost is paramount goal-N-R R-F: personal survival to fight an ally or friend-R: Picasso-R: picks nose covertly-N-R; picks nose overtly -NA (crass boor); "pillar of the community"-usually an A-R: pirate-RR: Pitt-R: platitudinous-A-R; Platypus-are you kidding?:

## CREATIVE INSUBORDINATION

plunges passionately into adventure-R; poseur-PS-R: possesses sufficient self-esteem to be unthreatened able to foster it in others-R; Powell-DAMN (Don't ask me. Norbert)-probably a Rebel at heart; Prohibitionist-A-R: promotes the distribution of condoms in schools-R with a lot of practical knowledge of human nature, particularly human teenage nature; proponent of "trickle down" economics-A-R: proponent of an unjust law-RA-R

# Q

Quayle-a recently (as of this writing) and blessedly unemployed A-R: Queen Guinevere-R: Queen Marie-Antoinette-A-R

# R

"radical-chic"-PS-R; radical Non-Rebel-OX; radical Rebel-RED; Ayn Rand R; ready to follow any rule, even ridiculous ones-N-R; Reagan-A-R; recognizes that sometimes it takes more courage not to fight-R; recognizes that no job is worth one's integrity-R; recognizes that the power of one's mission and message, and who one is inside, bear far more weight than one's clothing or hair style, etc.-R; recognizes that to dare is the highest wisdom-R: regards hypocrisy as the human mind's most vicious mechanism-R; religious funda mentalist who forces his dogma upon everyone else-A-R; relishes role of underdog-R; reluctant to follow anyone else's rules-R; reluctant to follow rules, period-RR; renegade-RR: repeatedly and pompously, etc.-PS-R.AR. or simply an a-- h--; restless soul who would rather go to Hell if it were lively than dreamily drift in Heaven-R; retains a spiritual reserve of resilient strength when under overwhelming attack-R; righteous but not self-righteous-R; Rivera-R; Rob Roy-R; Robertson-A-R (anyone who could seriously claim that then-President Bush was carrying out the mission of a group that wants a new world order "under the domination of Lucifer" has to be either an Anti Rebel or more than a little nuts, or both); Robeson, Paul-R; Robespierre-A-R; Robin Hood-R: Rogers-R: Romney, G.-R; Romney, M.-A-R: Roosevelt-R

# CREATIVE INSUBORDINATION

# S

Sakharov-R; Sandusky-NA, a monster; Sartre-R; Schindler-R; seeks out and associates with creative and imaginative people of any background or lifestyle-R; seeks to join the "right" sorority or fraternity-N-R: segregationist-A-R: self-righteous-A-R; self-serving lobbyist-RED; Shakespeare's "petty men who peep about to find themselves dishonorable graves"-N-R's: "sheep in sheep's clothing"-N-R's: "sheep in wolf's clothing"-PS-R's: Siegel -RR: Silver, Long Dong-R: Silver, Long John-R; Sinclair-R; Socrates-R: somehow changes world for the better-R; someone apt to have dog named "Checkers"-A-R: someone apt to have dog named "Cochise"-R or PS-R; someone apt to have dog named "Trixie"-N-R; someone not of Native American descent who constantly sports Native-American garb, or someone from the Northeastem part of the country who obsessively dresses Western

PS-R: someone quite likely to have a cat named "Dog"-R or PS-R; someone the author of this book needs to have around so he can have somebody to poke fun at once in a while-N-R; someone who is open to marriage or an overt liaison with a vibrant opposite-sex person of any race, class, or religion and doesn't care who knows about it, etc.-R; someone who would gladly go to bed with an attractive opposite-sex person of another race, class, or religion if nobody else knew about it-most likely an N-R; Spartacus-R; Spielberg-R: Springer-R; Steinbeck-R; Supreme Court Justice who thinks corporations are people-A-R: Sutton-RR; Swaggart-R A-R; Swift-R

# T

Taylor-I say R because she bucked the Hollywood trend by marrying half a dozen of her lovers, but some may argue she was an N-R because she deemed it necessary to marry them; "Teflon" individual marvelously adept at avoiding or shifting blame-N-R; tends to make most "pillars of the community" very uneasy-R; tends toward untidiness-R; the best lover-R, unquestionably; the eagle in the sky-R: the "Joker" as portrayed by Jack Nicholson-RR: the unique individual psyche's last romanticist-R; thinks women's primary reason for existence on this earth is to please men-A-R; Thomas-N-R (any black man who says he likes Mississippi because "they still sell those little pickaninny dolls down there-and I bought me a few of them, too" has to be a Non-Rebel); Thoreau-R: timid-N-R; treats beggars and kings just the same-R; tries, invariably, to vote with the majority-N-R; "tries not to think about it" as a psychologically repressive mechanism for coping with societal ills (and as a safe-sex practice)-N-R: Truman-R: truthful politician-OX Twain-R

## U

Unanue-R: uncontrollable-R: "underground"-R's; uses shock words to blast the barnacles off people and energize them to take positive reformative action-R

## V

values the vigor of slang and recognizes that it's created in a spirit of exuberant defiance-R; very tidy-usually an N-R; volunteers to picket... except on bowling night, etc.-S-R (Semi-Rebel)

## W

Wallace-R: Wallenberg-R: Washington-R: Wayne, John-A-R: Wayne Newton fan-probably an N-R; West, Cornel-R; West, Mae-R; Whoopi Goldberg-R; Wisian-N-A (doesn't exist); wolf in sheep's clothing-RR: wolf in wolf's clothing-A-R or RR; woman with sex trophies-NA (lunatic): Woodward & Bernstein-R's: would go to great lengths to prevent people ... from reading this book-A-R: would make a good... Nazi-N-R: would personally subdivide it and profit from it-N-R R-F: would standy by and let the Redwood Forest be cut down-N-R; Wright-R; Wylie-R

## X

X (Malcolm)-RR who reformed and grew to "R" status just before he was assassinated; xenophobe-A-R; xerxes-A-R

## Y

Yevtushenko R: you-probably R: your best friend-?: your favorite public figure, past or present-R, I would surmise; your least-favorite public figure probably in some classification other than "R"; your parents-?: your playmates who are playing this game with you-??: your "significant other"- probably either an R or a long-suffering N-R: your worst enemy, if you have one probably an A-R, an R A-R, or an N-R R-F

## Z

Zapata, a glorious R: Zimmerman-R A-R

# APPENDIX A

### Address of interim Superintendent-elect to Detroit Board of Education, July 12, 2012

**Excerpt of the text of my first formal address delivered to the Board of Education, on the occasion of my having taken a Board-appointed chair at the Board table as interim Superintendent-elect of the Detroit Public Schools on July 12, 2012.**

President Lemmons. Honorable Board Members, and Community Attendees:

I am honored to have been appointed by this democratically-elected Detroit Board of Education to the interim position of Superintendent of the Detroit Public Schools. President [Lamar] Lemmons has made me aware that he and this courageous Board have been undemocratically criticized in some quarters for naming a white man to this vital post, and Mr. Lemmons tells me he responded to one of these critics with this question: "Which would you rather have as your Superintendent of Schools-John Brown or Clarence Thomas?" I can assure you that historic abolitionist John Brown and I have considerably more in common than the two of us having happened to be born of free Scottish ancestry more than a century apart, as everyone soon will learn.

I am grateful to this Board for affording me the God-given chance to give something back to the school district that educated me and to show my gratitude to those long-dead DPS athletic coaches who turned me in the right direction in the very early 1950s, sixty-one years ago-when our school district was at the very peak of its powers. Those among you who have read my books know that in keeping with my hard-earned past professional reputation that was gained as an activist educator throughout the past half century and more of often extremely tumultuous years will do my utmost to serve our kids and our community at the same level of energy I spent when I was outrunning Olympic champions. I will also do this sacred job with the same crusading zeal that I manifested when I was racially integrating white suburban school-district administrative and instructional staffs and integrating suburban student populations when I was a deputy superintendent and super intendment there-and when as a recent executive director in Detroit I blew the whistle on incompetence and corruption at the top levels that now have finally brought us down to the despondent depths where we sit today.

Most Detroiters are aware that corporate-collusive Republicans in the state of Florida resorted to several undemocratic, dictatorial measures to put George W. Bush in the White House illegally in the year 2000. What followed was a mass-impoverishing, mendacious, treasonous, and murderous, eight-year presidential crime spree from which millions of ordinary Americans are yet to recover. These corporate-collusive Florida Republicans were aided and abetted in this infamous enterprise by a politically skewed United States Supreme Court that made that tragic Bush victory possible.

What still isn't as well known by too many of us here in Detroit is that on a nationwide basis, similarly corporate-collusive Republican legislators in Congress and in state capitol buildings all across our troublingly divided country are resorting to similarly fascistic, dictatorial measures in an effort to deprive countless numbers of African-Americans and other minority Americans of their voting rights in a racist and economically motivated effort to deny President Obama the second term that 99 percent of our fellow citizens desperately need him to have.

What is unfortunately even LESS known and LESS publicized (except in the Metro Times and in our battling little community newspapers like the Michigan Citizen and the Detroit Native Sun, and by a very few courageous major media print and television reporters such as Chastity Pratt of the Detroit Free Press and Huel Perkins of FoxTV2) is that the majority-Republican, corporate collusive Michigan Legislature is endeavoring to plunder and hijack our schools and our entire city right here in Detroit-and right out from under our very noses. I also tend to wonder whether some members of the [Roy] Roberts [Emergency Financial Management) administration may even hope that the Detroit Federation of Teachers goes out on strike in the fall so more children will be forced to enroll in the state's bogus and illegally created so-called "Educational Achievement" System. I will be dialoguing with Detroit Federation of Teachers President Keith Johnson to try to ensure that the DFT won't go on strike and thereby play right into the hands of the Roberts administration before I assume the duties of the interim Superintendence and I then am able to bargain with the teachers' union fairly and equitably as soon as I sit in that chair.

In the midst of all this, an appellate panel of three Republican judges recently and somewhat surprisingly did the right thing! They overruled an illegal decision fomented by the two Republican lackeys on the Board of Canvassers. That original undemocratic decision by the majority Republican state legislators' water-carriers on the politically split Board of Canvassers had sought to disqualify the petitions which were legitimately signed by a quarter million citizens in the righteous crusade to overturn Public Act 4-the infamous Emergency Manager Law (better known as the Emergency Dictator Law) and thus pave the way to place the challenge to that rogue, un-Constitutional law on the November ballot. The two Republican members had hypocritically effected this illegal decision on the preposterous pretext that the font size on the petitions was incorrect! The three judges' ruling thus did indeed pave the way for this democratically-elected Detroit school board to regain its full power! Accordingly, on Thursday, June 14, at its regularly-scheduled meeting, this board did indeed vote 7-2 to name me interim Superintendent elect of the Detroit Public Schools as duly reported in the Detroit Free Press the following day.

And as you know, to avoid any suspicion or accusation that I am accepting this job for any motive other than to support our Constitutionally-protected voting rights, to serve my home town district's public schoolchildren, and to set our school district on the right course toward its old-time excellence. I have opted to accept an annual salary of one single solitary dollar.

However, probably least-known by the majority of my fellow Detroiters is the disgraceful fact that the two Republicans who comprise one-half of the Board of Canvassers illegally and immorally managed to stall past the end of the fiscal year to follow the three judges' order to place the challenge to the illegal Public Act 4 on the ballot. Had they placed Public Act 4 on the ballot, this act would have immediately rendered me your interim Superintendent. That stalling beyond June 30 which the Board of Canvassers did will now make it very difficult for me to reverse some of the damaging decisions that have been made recently by the Roberts administration without my resorting to time-consuming and expensive court action. These illegal decisions included the giving away of fifteen of Detroit's public schools to the bogus, new, so called "state-wide" Educational Achievement System. One of these schools was Denby High School, my alma mater. Two of them were Southeastern and Pershing-two high schools with long and distinguished histories, and also two schools where I coached and taught in the 1960s. These illegal decisions also involved the closing of other DPS schools. One of them that is being closed and sold is the grand old Southwestern High, where I also coached and taught, and where hundreds of thousands of dollars that were levied upon us Detroit taxpayers were spent last year to build a modern new track facility.

These illegal decisions have also included changing the name of a high school named for the Finney family of abolitionists (Finney being a school where I also coached and taught, and where in 2003 they named the track after me).

Inevitably now, we will need to undertake costly litigation to recoup all of these criminal thefts.

These illegal decisions on the part of the Roberts administration also included the dictatorial imposition of unfair, undemocratic, and draconian contractual measures that have been inflicted upon the Detroit Federation of Teachers and other DPS employees and bargaining groups.

Amid all of this, the Board of Canvassers had stubbornly continued to stall, and it would have done so for as long as it could possibly for as long as until August 27. Happily, the Michigan Supreme Court has now decided to hear the case involving the Republicans' ridiculous protest regarding the allegedly improper font size on the petitions regarding the citizens' challenge to PA 4 on this coming July 25, and the Court will have no moral and Constitutional choice but to follow legal precedent regarding such cases and accordingly rule that PA 4 will go on the November 6 ballot, which upon such ruling will immediately re-empower the elected but currently illegally disempowered Detroit School Board. So, fortunately for American Constitutional democracy but somewhat less happily for me personally, since July 25 may now undoubtedly be the latest date when the Supreme Court will rule on the case-it's evident that I won't become interim Superintendent any earlier than July 26, on which date (or perhaps on a date even later into August) will then be placed in the challenging position of having thus to assume belatedly the duties of interim Superintendent at some tardy point when Detroit public schools will be about to open! It is my very real and worrisome fear that I will therefore assume those duties just in time to encounter the same sort of disorganization and chaos that accompanied the opening of school last year and the year before. with kids holding-penned in auditoriums for many days, and with insufficient numbers of staff assigned to the schools, and with sixty or more students in a class.

I do however hope that those who are doing the present planning for the opening of school won't botch it the way they have done previously. I need to re-emphasize that aside from sharing my expertise with my hometown school district that educated me in the 1940s and '50s, a visceral reason for my agreeing to accept this challengingly Olympian job is the frightening fact that the powers granted to the Emergency Manager under Public Act 4, which voters will likely and rightfully reject in November, grossly exceed constitutionally required safeguards to protect our democratic form of government. Thus as a freedom-loving Detroiter and Michiganian and American, cannot agree with the scope of those powers, nor will I exercise in form or substance any of those dictatorial powers in performing my duties as interim Superintendent.

I do expect to perform the duties of interim Superintendent between an indefinite date late in the summer and the November 6 presidential election (and probably beyond the election, since Public Act 4 will almost certainly be defeated by the voters in this presidential election year, with the resultant heavy voter turnout in Detroit). Depending on how late in the summer the challenge to Public Act 4 goes on the ballot-and if it actually doesn't go on the ballot until as late as August 27-the timelines for my plans to put the machinery in place for the ultimate restoration of the Detroit Public Schools' one-time excellence will need to be adjusted accordingly.

All of this having been said, now I'd like to share some of my immediate and also my longer-term plans and observations with you.

Author's note: Here follows a reduced list of what originally were twenty three goals I shared with the Board:

ONE: As soon as President Lemmons has arranged for an initial meeting site for the Superintendent Candidate-Selection Committee, I will convene the Committee-and we will cooperatively devise a process for choosing candidates for the Board to interview and select to succeed me in the permanent job.

TWO: Both before and after school is safely underway, I will visit as many schools and classrooms as I can on a daily basis for the duration of my time in office.

THREE: I will meet with municipal, state, and Congressional elected officials, as well as with present and past members of the Detroit School Board, with business and community leaders, with college and university leaders, and with local pastors. I will seek their counsel and enlist their assistance in planning and helping to implement our course of action. I will also establish telephone and email contact with superintendents of urban districts of similar size to share ideas for district enhancements and for problem-solving.

FOUR: I then will begin to establish my plan for the Detroit Public Schools' long-overdue reformation. This plan will include the who/what/when/why and how components of accomplishing it, and it will include the recruitment of retired educators and educational administrators like me and practitioners of other professions (e.g., Business and Law), plus several community activists, to come in voluntarily and work pro bono, or for one dollar per annum, as I will be doing, and as attorney Thomas Bleakley has already done in drawing up my contract at the direction of Board President Lemmons. This plan will also include my deliberations regarding which top DPS administrative staff will be retained in their jobs (or strategically re-assigned to alternative jobs) and which ones won't be.

The plan will include, as well:

FIVE: the re-institution of fair collective bargaining for all bargaining groups. Relatedly, this will include paying earned sick days to union retirees who didn't get them, and it will include as well the affording of appropriate remuneration to those DPS staff who are on long-term disability. (Rather than putting some deserving staff on long-term disability, it has come to my attention that both recent and current DPS administrations have fired some such staff out-of-hand in callous disregard of contractual law, and I intend to determine the identity of these unfairly-treated staff members and restore their rightful benefits.)

SIX: The re-institution of Ebonics-anecdotal instruction in the English and Social Studies curricula;

SEVEN: The re-affirming of legally-mandated programs for special-needs students, including hearing-impaired students, and for students who speak English as their second language;

EIGHT: The re-hiring of the attendance officers, so they can round up the thousands of kids who during the past couple of years haven't been attending school anywhere:

NINE: The re-hire of former DPS in-school security officers who know the kids and who in the past have helped to keep the peace in the secondary schools and have been a potent force in ensuring that all of our students are safe in every one of our schools;

TEN: The crafting of an anti-nepotism and anti-cronyism hiring and promotion policy:

ELEVEN: The creation and re-creation of extensive, separately-housed alternative programs, the reduction of the class sizes in Grades One and Two.

and a squeezing of the financial "balloon" to provide for smaller class sizes and remediation in reading and enhanced social work service for temporarily exiled misbehavers at the secondary level;

TWELVE: The preparation of a plan to go to court to get the fifteen un Constitutionally hijacked schools back into the DPS fold;

THIRTEEN: A very close collaboration with the Mayor's office to keep school buildings and some remaining recreation centers (partially staffed with volunteers) open at night year-round for recreation and remediation;

FOURTEEN: The re-institution of an evaluation process for all staff and other involved persons, up to and including the interim Superintendent himself and the Board of Education itself;

FIFTEEN: The establishment of a more robust and district-wide parent organization with a true and heeded voice, and the rehire of the parent/ community liaison staff, in concert with a relevant parent/grandparent/guardian education component to reverse more than twenty years of mis-education of large numbers of former DPS students who now are DPS parents and grandparents:

SIXTEEN: The initiation of legal action to recover the approximately $340 million the state owes us that the state-engendered "reform" administrations squandered away during the past decade and more, including the surplus that was extant in 1999, plus interest; and

SEVENTEEN: The undertaking of a forensic financial audit.

All of the preceding (original 23 Goals], of course, represent less than half of the more crucial projects and problems that will need to be addressed.

I will open the financial records to the public and keep a wide-open door to the public, as well as an open door to my office for parent and community leaders and for the media, all of whose questions I will respond to within 48 hours, and sooner in an emergency. Then-in fair and honest cooperation with stakeholders (parents, teachers, students, principals, community leaders. business leaders, elected officials, service groups, et al.)-I will determine how best to expend funds thriftily for the good of the students' education.

What I definitely WON'T be spending any funds on are outside consultative "experts," multiple conferences and "retreats" at hotels outside (or inside) the city, or on airplane and cab fare and lodging and food bills for junkets to conferences in faraway places, or for a salary for me, or for a car and driver for me or my top aides, or for bodyguards for me or my top aides.

In closing, let me say that a visceral point for all of us to bear in mind (and be eternally thankful for) is that as this elected Board regains its citizen designated policy-determinant role and its right to appoint and evaluate a Superintendent of Schools who will serve at its pleasure, the rule of Constitutional law and the salvation of representative democracy will have been righteously restored in Detroit and Michigan.

# APPENDIX B

*Front page, Detroit Native Sun,*
*August 10, 2012*

## DETROIT Native Sun

**SPECIAL POLITICAL ISSUE**

## RETURN TO POWER

### New superintendent to lead exiled DPS Board back to the promised land

By Valerie D. Lockhart
SUN EXECUTIVE EDITOR

Just as Moses rescued the Israelites from the oppressive hands of Pharaoh and boldly declared, "Let my people go," a similar demand may soon be uttered by Detroit Public School's interim superintendent, Dr. John Telford, to free the troubled school system and its exiled board from the grip of an Emergency Manager and to lead them back to the Promised Land.

"I'm smart and fearless. I say it without arrogance. Its fact," says Telford, a civil rights activist, former DPS executive and teacher, athlete and superintendent of the Rochester and Madison Heights Public School districts. "I will do my utmost to serve our kids and our community at the same level of energy I spent when I was outrunning Olympic champions. I will also do this sacred job with the same crusading zeal that I manifested when I was racially integrating white suburban school-district administrative and instructional staffs and integrating suburban student populations, when I was a deputy superintendent and superintendent there, and when as a recent executive director in Detroit, I blew the whistle on incompetence and corruption at the top levels that now have finally brought us down to the despondent depths where we sit today."

Seeking to dig themselves out of a hole created by incompetence and corruption, the exiled board outwitted EM Roy Roberts,

-- See RETURN TO POWER page 5

# ACKNOWLEDGMENTS

(Note: To avoid rendering the Acknowledgments longer than this tooth some tome itself, I apologize for having to leave out hundreds of colleagues, compares, students, and athletes who at some point within the past three quarters of a century affected my life profoundly, and more than enough to merit inclusion on this list. For the same reason, I have left out all of the numerous titles-"Dr." for "Doctor," "Rev." for "Reverend," "Col." for "Colonel," "Sen." for "Senator," etc.-before the names of the numerous acknowledged folk who hold or held these distinguished titles.)

This having been said, I gratefully wish to cite (mostly in non-preferential order) those many persons alive and dead who in one way or another helped inspire me in my lifelong Creatively Insubordinate Crusade against pervasive injustices. Many of them also shared with me their precious friendship and love.

(Incidentally, I've done my best to crowd as many of you wonderful folks in here as feasible so you'll buy the book and get copies for all your friends and order my other entrancing tomes, too, if you haven't got them already.)

These extraordinary people include my late, great, and long-lamented parents John and Helen Telford, my lovely wife Adrienne, my son Steven D. Telford, my daughter Katherine Fay Helen Telford Garrett, my son-in-law Rich Garrett, my grandchildren RJ and Victoria, my aunts Letty Telford, Margaret Telford Myers, Ann Boudro, Evelyn Johnson, and Mary Louise Fetter, my uncles Carl Boudro and Al Fetter, my cousin Jeff Telford and his gracious wife Betsy, my Second and Third Musketeer cousins and lifelong partners-in-assorted mischief Carl and Dick Boudro, Carl's widow Ginny, my godson Rick Boudro and his four interscholastic wrestling champion sons RJ, Paul, Brian, and Ben who followed in his footsteps, my uncle Frank Telford and aunt May, my mother's friend since childhood Margaret Johnson, my swift WSU teammate and close friend

# CREATIVE INSUBORDINATION

Cliff Hatcher, his son Marty, his wonderful wife Barbara, my marvelous goddaughter Joy Hatcher Chambers, my grand goddaughters Summer and Kyla, my friend of 75 years Dick Otten and his lovely wife JoAnn, and Daniel Telford, the gentle uncle I never knew.

Also, my legendary college coach David Lynn Holmes and his helpful wife Hazel, his son David L. Holmes Jr., brother Carl, daughter Jean Wunderlich. nephews Robert and Lynn Holmes, and grandson Keith Wunderlich, my high school coaches Ralph Green and Jack Rice, and my boxing trainer Tom Briscoe.

Also, all of my good and true friends-George and Joyce Blaney, their stalwart sons Gregg. Jeff, and Adam; Char Blaney, Doris Blaney. Jerome J. Catalina (the Catman) and his hurdling brother Tim, "Bullet Billy" Smith, Paul and Orlin Jones, Ralph Carter, Pete and Lois Petross and their devoted daughter Candace, Robert Plumpe, Jim and Martha Bibbs, Robert Landry and kissin' cousin Lisa, Dick "Night Train" Lane, Detroit Olympians Lorenzo Wright. Henry Carr, and Eddie Tolan, big Charlie McIntosh, Matthew and Victoria King. Darius Morris, Anthony Neely, Sam and Marilyn Flam, Joltin' Joe Haddad, Karen Haddad Balog, and my great national and international track compadres Glenn Davis, Charley Jenkins, George Rhoden, Mike Larrabee, Hayes Jones, Les Carney, Jerry Welbourn, Dave Owens, Bill Duckworth, Ernie Shelton, Elias Gilbert. Ernie Shelby, Josh Culbreath, Mal Spence, Ira Murchison, Reggie Pearman, Hugo Maiocco, Bob McMurray, Rex Cawley, Bill Crothers, Lang Stanley, John Bork, Jack Yerman, Frank Bowens, Pete Orr, Leonard Lyles, Billy Cannon, Jim Brown, Dave Mills, Livio Berruti, Giovanni Scavo, and lost U.S. Olympian Cliff Cushman, whose fighter plane got shot down over Cambodia defending our country from Vietnamese peasants for the military/industrial complex.

Also, Metro Detroit TV2 Anchor Huel Perkins, Michigan Governor Jennifer Granholm, Detroit Mayors Coleman Young and Dennis Archer, Congressmen John Conyers and Hansen Clarke, Heaster Wheeler, Wendell Anthony, Nicholas Hood III, Dan White, Rhonda Walker, Carol Klenow, Gary Doyle, Bob Wingo. Leon Wingo, Buddy Coleman, Jim Plath, Stan Stankovich, Arkles and Sarah Brooks, Bill King, Steve and Gerri Rhoads,

Carl and Marilyn Wagner, Richard and Virginia Starkey, Oscar Jones and his son Baxter, Charlie Purnell, Obra Purnell, Kevin and Ingrid Haywood, Margot Owens, Alayna Mike, Frank Mike, Joe and Linda Dupree, Duane and Sally Hull, Dick Turco, Greg and Sue Owens. John Kitchen, George Wesson, Mark Zurek, Dennis Turner, Henry Gerstheimer, John Saddler, George Fancy, Wayne Dyer, Ken and Connie Howse, Hiram and Judy Badia, David Rambeau, Art Robbie, Henry Hank, Ruben Wilson, Tom and Dreena Jones, Yusef Shakur, Larry and Susan Laconis, Mark H. Smith, Ron Hunter, Elliott Haskins, Jeanne and Jerry Bocci, Tim Moore, Diann Woodard, Dan Krichbaum, Daedra McGhee, Avery Jackson, Jr., Wright Mitchell, Beverly Kindle-Walker, Muhammad Alif. Frank Carissimi, Tom and Mary Ellen Bleakley. Robert Hanna, Charlie and Lois Primas, Freddie Prime, Ron Teasley, Jerry Bell, Willie Yee, Frank and Angela McBride, Josh Bassett, Jim and Mary Bleakley, Bill and Pat Richer, Al Bequette, Ken Pringle, Bob Fabris, Robert Morris, Joe Hudson, Shawon Respress, Julie Telang, David Pryor, Bob Thomas, Ray and Demetrius Wright, Tim and Kyria Gore, Alford G. Harris, and my buddies from way back in kindergarten at old Estabrook School, Billy Flowers and Clyde Sanford, and also Nora Murphey.

Also, former Team for Justice president Thomas Randolph III, crusading attorneys Bernie Fieger and his son Geoffrey, Jim Jacobs, Don Frederickson. Bill Stewart, Keith Williams, Dave Snead, Jim and Pat Solomon, Stephanie Rivers, Lavonne Sheffield, Ron Peart, Barry Ross, Harry Cook. Tom Watkins. Chet Wydrinsky, Ines de Jesus, Robert Chiarini, Don and Rhonda Falkenbury, Linda Yaden, Dennis Prost, Earl Kelley, Pam Flanigan, Danny Moss, Ken Donaldson, Nick and Christine Cheolas, Dennie Ewell. William Ewell, William Sharp, Sharon Davis, Bill Hoth, Samuel Golden, Danny and Lisa Applefield, Danny Watkins, Liz and Jerry Walters, Sheldon Applefield, Paul Maloney, Paris "Sandy" Whittington, George Brown, Tarp London. Heaster Wheeler, Ernie Wagner, Janae Allen, Robert Henderson. Tyisha Mills, Ray Slack, A'Daisha Pickett, Keith Walton, Sironte Williams, Orelia Brown, Tony Merritt. Arlandis Lawrence. Clyde Cleveland, Roland Brown, Wayne Tuff, Dominique Harris, Yvonne Walker. Ilene Ingram, Malik Shabazz, Bob and Shirley Peters. Diane Stewart, Julie Zboril, Sheila Schmittel. Danjetta Driver, Ronda Reaver, Te-Rahn Williams, Dean Parker, Anjela Banks,

Donetta Mitchell, Lamont Smith. Jamaal Thornton, Jeffrey and Missy May, Bill and Carol Breen, Reggie and Cynthia Bradford, Bob Gutow, Sergio Ramirez, Thomas and Christopher Chastain, Bob Moore, Ron

Karvonen, and Ron's intrepid sister Joan.

Also, Geraldine Natalie Barclay, Mel and Roslyn Barclay, Joe and Rachel Barclay, Joshua Barclay, Bill Lipson and Greta Barclay Lipson and their sons Eric, Mark and Steve, Ken and Kimberly Cockrel, Gary and Sandi Faber, James Moriarty, Kenyetta Wilbourn, Bob and Marietta Samaras, JoAnn Podoczak, Walt and Jackie Bartnick, John and Dolores Schultz, Alvin and Rae Ward, Dale Hardeman, Keith Johnson, Margery Readhead, Edwin Rowe, Stan Fields, Al Zack. Matt Lee, Kevin Johnson, Tommy Sledge, Ed Kozlov, Maggie DeSantis, Mike Whitty, Mike Wilmot, George Gaines, Dick Brown, John Lee, George Gaddy. Tom Cleveland, Ronnie Phillips, Mike Liebler, Ken and Betty Hines, Ken and Eileen Burnley, Lloyd Carr, Patrick and Patricia Dignan, and Spencer Haywood.

Also, Glenn Doughty, Toni Nicholas, Sam and Marilyn Flam, Dick Lobenthal, john powell, Barbara Powell, Gil Woodcock, Shirley Woodcock Gottschalk, Leroy Strayhorn, Michael Morris, Bob Kemp, Gracie Kemp, Sierra Smith, Alex Shami, Hilmer Kenty, Marv Rubin, Jerry and Sharron Freeman, Keith and Marian McClellan, Robert Plumpe, Margaret "Peggy" Tatham and her daughters Jeanne and Evelyn, Alberta and Colette Witherspoon, Carlos Lopez, Warren London. John Kline, Gene Kline, James Lee, Katie Yeager Hutchings Herzog Pridonoff, Steve Stonebreaker, Andy and Kathy Guest, Aaron and Sandra Gordon, and former Detroit mayor Kwame Kilpatrick (yes, the incarcerated Kwame-his "better angel" influenced me, too).

Also, Judith Urban and her daughter Kellie and son-in-law George Rouhib, Jim and Christine Campitelle, Nabila Shami, Leroy Dues, Charlie and Lois Primas. Will Robinson, Ron and Alecia Turner, Bill Wagner, Roger Byrd, Kelly Conway. Dan Conway, Bill and Gerry Keane, Jim Jacobs, Terry and Ruth Follbaum. Janina Jacobs, Diane Stuart, Bob and Shirley Peters, Pam and Keith Owens, Keith Wittenstrom, Robert and Judy Wollack, Roy Allen, Stan and Mattie Allen, Deborah Anthony. Jon Lockard and Jon Jr., Ken Riley, Chris Imber, Eric McKeon, George

Gaines, Mark Risch, Shireese Statin, Corey Stedman, Joel Sellentine, Wyatt Harris, Monique Baker-McCormick, Sherry Gay-Dagnogo, John and Peggy Dougherty, Dan Banks, Lem Barney, Sam Barresi, Dan Badia, Norm Lippett, Richard Bernstein, Russ Bellant, Stan Bell, Josh Bassett, Curtis Ivery, Peter Bernard, Tula Bazeos, Murel Bartley, Bill and Carol Breen, Tim Brooks, Craig Bryson, George Blaha, Bill Bowles, Bob Boyce, Charles Boyce, Ulysses Boykin. Jim and Christine Campitelle, Annie Carter, Stan Childress, Bruce Sullivan Feaster. Juanita Clay Chambers, Paris McCloud, Jody Cohen, Ronald Coleman, Bill Brooks. Betty Davis, Dan Grasschuk, John Harris, Cheryl Harshaw, Linda Spight, Ellen Stephens, Claude Tiller, Terry Truvillion, Ingrid Rhodes, Monica Johnson. Deborah Omokehinde, Charldine Bowens, Kai Johnson, Freddie Payne, Adnan Khalil, Kenny Vue, Minnie Pearce, Elijah Ross, Tommie Burton, Maurice Cochran, Mary Redmond, Annie Carter, Ida Short, Paula Johnson, Marchel McGehee, Janice McClellan, Felecia Tyson, LaToshia Love, Natalie Vaughn, Marshall Dickerson, Diana Dillaber Murray, Arthur Divers, Jimmy Dixon, Gary Doyle, Karen Dumas, Bob Dupuis, Ron Dzwonkowski. Sherman Eaton, Eddie and Mary Edwards, and Natalie Jacobson.

Also, Dingding Feng, Karyn Brantley-Johnson, Keenann Knox, Maureen Meuser, Perry Munson, Alvin Sims, Ernestine Smith, Stan Tinsley, Tracy Thomas, Phil Williams, Jerry and Lynn Morris, David Badger, Emmanuel Ivey, Elijah Coleman, Shanel Burgan, Chauncey Holdby, Quillan Curtin, Norman Pitts, Portia Gandy, Calvin James, Alwarithun Maquaribu, Via Weary, Calvin Trent, Doreen Turk-White, Mike Flanagan, Janice Frazier, Dave Fukuzawa, Helen Suchara, Ted Talbert, Mike Tenbusch and his father John, Kevin Gafford, Brenda Gatlin, Ronnie Bradshaw, Paul and Sylvia Garbe, Jane Garcia, Charles Dukes, Robert Glenn, Lew Schulman, Nate Goldberg, Sigrid Grace, Herman Gray, Karl Gregory, Harry and Martha Thomalla, Greg Thrasher, Dale Yagiela, Elliott Hall, Rich Halladay, Earl and Joyce Harrington. Janet Stankowsky, Rhoda Havrelock, Hal Schram, Zeline Richard, Freman Hendrix, Kim Heron, Vernell Simmons, Benne Smith, Agnes Hitchcock, Bill Hoover, Willie Horton, Larry Hudas, Ralph and Audrey Hutchings, Elbert Richmond, Dannie Ervine, Wayne Stewart, Donald Storey, Moses "Bill" Yearby, Claude Young, Chuck Smith, Dennis Zimmer, Sam Riddle,

# CREATIVE INSUBORDINATION

Amy Jadallah, Jim Jacobs, Arthur Jefferson, Doyle Johnson, Barnett Jones, John Kastran, Dave Hurst, Gail Kearns, Marge Stoi, Bianca Suarez, Bonnie Manhart, Vince and Izzy Khapoya, and Cyrus Webb of Mississippi.

Also, Anthony Adams, Lawrence Hemingway, Anita Koch, John Korachis. Al Silber, Bill Laitner, Pauline Leatherwood, Charley Rice, Bill and Tony Lipuma. Chuck Lewis, Pete Walsh, Robert Solari, Shirley and George Spaniel, John Vavruska, Henry Stallings, Alonzo Littlejohn, Dave Lister, Ruth Barry, Orian Worden, Bob Petti, Drake Wilkins, Linda Washington-Peoples, Lou Scott, Sue Barron, Scott Johnson, Sharon Kline, Ron Malis, Don Canham, Toney Manson, Mel Blohm, Doug Martens, Jeff Sternberg, Dave Mattingly, Connie Martinson. Sam McCargo, Stewart McMillin, Michael Jackman, Andy Meisner, Ron Mets. Leland Stein, Ralph Richardson, Doug Mobley, Donnell White, Steve Spreitzer, Jeff and Bridgett Nelson, Tom Nelson, Sy Gretchko. Bev Nettles-Nickerson, Michelle Rhea, Brad Edwards, Stuart Filler, Sylvia Hubbard, Mike Williams, Tom Northey, Mary Otten, Ed Page, Fred Pearson, Charles Span, Donna Thornton, John and Evelyn Petty, Marsha Pickens. Andy Rio, Ray Scott, Geno Pirrami, Mildred Williams, Tom Watkins, Bo Schembechler, Wardell Montgomery, Ruben Porter, Dave Points, Dennis Prost. Mike "Tiger" Price, Karen Quarnstrom, James E. Ray, Pat Richardson, Mark and Jenny Woliung, T. C. Roekle, Minnie and Cory Phillips, Maryann Webb, Cliff Russell, Jack Sada, Isabel Salas, Oliver Sanders, Gertrude Satterwhite, Matt Schatmeyer, Franklin and Jean Dohanyos, Rudy Serra, Doris Reese, Glenn Martin, Ed Simpkins, Karen Simmons, Arnold Smedes, Robert Shumake, Ted Talbert, Rachel Tiseo, Carson Tutt, Bruce Waha, Irwin Vance, Donna Tsegai-Vinson, Deb Walter, Sandra Overstreet Ware, Mary Chapman, Sam Washington, Larry Westley, Brenda Wellons-Watson, Rob Fournier, Joe Babb, Larry Weisman, Mike Shewach, Freddie Williams, Ernie Winchester, Lucius Cotton, and Jimmie Ward.

Also, Ceil Mrock, Eleanor White, Paul Seal, Carol Mims-Foster, Gene Seaborn, Luther Keith, Hugh Burrell, Sherry Cudillo, Corinna Ditta, Albert Lorenzo, Edna Smith, Julie Zboril, Pauline Badge, Edith Latham, Dale Hardeman, Paul Cabell, Terry Cabell, Cornelius Fortune, Bill and Dodie Waun, Monifa Jumanne, Elaine Gorzelski, Dave Gorzelski, Colleen McRorie, Jeff Ferguson, Hugh and Yoonsil Gersch. Norm and Oksana

Urban, Roy Burkhart, Vernita Samantha White, Angeline Urban Pryor, my first and second wives Lynn and Gina, my cousin Judy Telford Ballantyne, my cousin Ruth Ann Johnson McGee McCarty Hibbard Lowenthal, Tommy Sledge, my cousins Janet Bushor, Beverly Arce, and Billy Brown, my cousin Marchita Telford Fodor Blaske and her husband Bob and sons Gary and Rob and daughter Pat, my cousin Christy and her husbands Jerry DeRosa and Kim Geake and sons Jerry, Jr. and Richard Geake, my grandparents Frank and Margaret Telford and Perry and Christine Mark. my cousin Jeff Telford's high-achieving offspring John Telford and Jeff, Jr. and Judy and Kathy, my uncle Jimmy and Aunt Dorothy Mark and their offspring Doreen, Peter, Tommie, Kaaaren, and Douglas, my cousin Susan Boudro Gibson and her husband Ray, my cousins Jack Daniels and Diane Boudro Miller, and my dad's cousins Danny Carle and Alex and Jimmy Carlin.

I love or have loved you all.

In addition, at the risk of making the List of Acknowledgments stretch interminably longer than this battling and embattled book itself, need to add my loyal and loving mutt Rap (Rapscallion) for backing me up in boyhood brawls and for fetching us the morning newspaper from neighbors' porches.

Further, I would like to mention our venerable tabby Thurstine, who put up semi-patiently with my and my daughter's "cat hunts" around the house for twenty years, and our smart calico Whitleigh and her not-as-smart but equally beautiful sable sister, Samantha. I also choose to include my well fanged black feline Little Never-Full and his predatory brothers and sisters and sleek, sable mother cat for keeping the rat population somewhat in check at 6021 Sixteenth Street at McGraw in central Detroit throughout the 1940s.

I also choose to include two additional mutts-big, protective Kyra (part German Shepherd) and frenetic little Bee-Bee (a Pomeranian mix)- who fully reconfirmed my lifelong love for the canine species..

Finally, I mustn't overlook one large, long-haired, pugnacious, black female feline named Mindy. Her lightning-fast paws re-taught your old author how to box, albeit a relatively useless skill on some teeming streets in my hometown, whereupon AK 47's proliferate, usually in the wrong hands. This proliferation confirms the need now more than ever for Creative Insubordination—the vigilante version or perhaps the need for an ultimate recruitment of the bad guys themselves to join what sadly may soon become an imminent revolution. Creative Insubordination and insurrection on a national scale happened in Scotland and France and Haiti and Mexico and Russia and Cuba and in many other oppressed countries, including this one in 1776. If the crocodilian corporate criminals and their legislative and judicial henchmen don't "wake up and smell the coffee" pretty damn soon, instead they're going to wake up one cataclysmic day and smell the gunpowder.

# INDEX

**A**

ACLU  viii, 36

A Life on the RUN (book)  21, 27, 37, 40, 49, 60, 81, 145

American Revolution  10

Amin, Idi  80, 92

Army of the Confederacy, U.S. Civil War  80

Arnold, Benedict  80

ASCD (Association of Supervisors of Curriculum Development)  48

**B**

Bakker, Jim  80, 92

Bernstein, Leonard  79, 93

Bieber, Justin  79, 93

Billings, Montana  10, 11

Black Panthers (political party)  79, 81, 145

Boehner, John  67

Boggs, Grace Lee  x, 46

Boxing (the "Sweet Science")  82

Boyne Mountain, Michigan  48

British Army  70

British Crown  10

Brotherhood Unit  40, 41

Burns, Robert  x, 35

Burr, Aaron  80

Bush, George H. W.  64, 80, 93

Bush, George W.  64, 93, 108, 119

**C**

Caesar, Julius  19, 103

Caligula  80

Campitelle, James  43

Chapman, Sgt. Walter  75, 76

Chastain, Thomas  131

Churchill, Winston  54, 69, 78, 94

Clay, Andrew Dice  78, 94

Coolidge, Calvin  14

Couch, Earl  50

Creative Insubordination: Defined  1, 4, 7, 8

**D**

Danish Jews  11

Dark Ages  v, 84

Democrat  v, 18, 59, 77, 83, 99, 112

Demo publicans  66

Denmark  11
  King of  11

Detroit, city of  xiv

Detroit Free Press  v, xiv, 22, 41, 119, 120

Detroit Native Sun (newspaper)  xiii, 119, 127, 145

Detroit Public School Board  72, 120, 145, 147

Detroit Public Schools  vi, viii, xiv, xv, 4, 21, 41, 59, 72, 73, 118, 120, 123, 144

DiBiaggio. John  17, 18

Dickenson, Emily  x, 23, 94

## E

Eisenhower, Dwight D.  18

Engler, John  22

Exclusionary real estate covenants  2

## F

Finney High School, Detroit  86, 145

Finn, Huckleberry (fictional character)  40, 47

Flynn, Errol  80, 95

Franklin, Benjamin  ix, 10, 95

Frost, Robert  x, 23, 55, 96

## G

Gingrich, Newt  67, 108

Goldenberg, Oren  46

Graves, Peter  77

Grosse Point, Michigan  72

Guevara, Che  ix, 80, 96

## H

Hart Middle School, Rochester, Michigan  44

Hatcher, Cliff  29, 129

Hayes, Woody  17

Highland Park, Michigan  75

Hines, Betty  54, 131

Hitler, Adolf  80, 97

Holmes, David L.  9, 10, 129

Huckleberry Finn (book)  40

## I

Indiana University  17

## J

Jackson, Jr.. Avery  xix, 49, 130

Jamaica  10

Jenkins, Charley  10, 45, 129

Jesus Christ  98

Jim Crow laws  2

Jurassic Park  12, 84

## K

Keating, Charles  80, 98
Kennedy, John F.  3, 82, 98
Kennedy, Robert F  ix, 71, 98
King, Jr., Martin Luther  ix, 71, 98, 112
Kipling, Rudyard  56
Kirschenbaum, Stuart  vi, 22, 36
Knight, Bobby  17, 98
Korean War  18
Kozma, Thomas William  61

## L

Larrabee, Mike  10, 129
Lassie (dog)  78
Lauren, Iowa  43
Lincoln, Abraham  71
Lindsay, Vachel  56

## M

MacArthur, Douglas  18
Machiavelli, Nicolo  1, 48
Madison District Public schools  86
Matthews, Vince  10, 45
McGrath, Coleen  39
McGrath, Mary  38
McKenley, Herb  84

Metropolitan Detroit Youth Foundation  47, 68
Michigan National Guard  72
Michigan State Boxing Commission  22
Michigan State University  17
Moore, Joyce  54
Mother Teresa  ix, 68
My Race Be Won (book)  10, 45

## N

NAAU (National Amateur Athletic Union)  45
Nazi Germany  1
NCAA (National Collegiate Athletic Association): All-American Team  17, 29, 45, 144
Nero  80
Nevada  44
News Talk 1200 AM Detroit  73
New York Philharmonic Orchestra  79
North Africa  70
North, Oliver  80, 100

## O

Oakland University  48, 57
Obama, Barack H.  xix, 3, 100, 119
Oldham, Mike  12

Olympic Games (reference) 84
O'Neill-Pottery, Helen 43

**P**

PACS (political action committees) 71
Parker, Dorothy ix, 14, 101
Paterno, Joe 17
Pennsylvania State University 17
Perles, George 17
Persian Gulf War 37
Petross, Irving "Pete" 28, 129
Plymouth, Michigan 38
Poems
  1 Brake for Animals 63
  A Christmas Card c/o the Wayne County Jail 64
  A Curse Upon the Creature Who Killed the Little Girl 65
  Addiction-Affliction Friction 24
  A Dirge for Karolyn & Me 23
  America. My Love 63
  Bush & Cheney 63
  Comes the Revolution 66
  For Cliff Hatcher 29
  For Katie 26
  For My Big Blond Cousin Carl 31
  For Peggy 25
  For Scotty 35
  For Steve 35
  For Tori 34
  In a Baghdad Alley 64
  My Silent Violin 33
  Obama Be Praised 57
  O Bronco That Would Not Be Broken of Dancing 56
  On the Passing of Pete Petross 28
  Rex Reborn 6
  Salvaging My Soul 69
  Sixteenth Street. 1970 28
  Something Tranquil 24
  Sonnet for a Safer Sea 6
  The Ancient Blood Code 74
  The Creative Old Crusader's Credo 56
  The Push button Prayer 5
  The Third Wife 27
  The Thirteenth Hour 7
  Unstarlit 32
  Wanda-Lust (reference) 27
Pol Pot 80
Puscas, George 22

**Q**

Quarter-miling 45

**R**

Reagan, Ronald 18, 102

Republicans 4, 11, 59, 78, 80, 119, 120, 121

Reuther, Walter 51

Rhoden, George 10, 84, 85, 129

"Rig" (quarter-miling reference) 8

Rin Tin Tin (dog) 78

Rochester Community Schools, Michigan 40, 61

Rochester Hills, Michigan 43, 72

Rome 19, 30, 31

Roosevelt, Eleanor 71, 103

Rose Bowl 12

Royal Canadian Mounted Police 72

## S

Santorum, Rick 2

Schindler, Oskar 48, 103

Schwarzenegger, Arnold 18

Shakur, Yusef x, 56, 130

Southern California Striders 10

Southwestern High School, Detroit xix, 41, 49, 54, 75, 86

Stalin, Josef 80

Star of David, 11 Superintendency, Detroit Public Schools 11

St. George 11, 84

Straight, Alvin 43

Superintendency, Madison District Public Schools 86

Swigard, Kathy 44

Swigard, Steve 44

## T

Teapartiers 57

Telford, Frank Sr. and Margaret ("Maggie") Scottish grandparents of the author 70, 134

Telford, Jeffery Sr. and Jr. 45

Telford, Katherine x, 5, 128

Telford's Telescope (newspaper column) vi, 21, 73

The Longest Dash (book) 9, 10, 16, 45, 144

The Metro Times 28, 119

The Michigan Chronicle vi, vii, xviii, 21, 73

The Ohio State University 17

The Window 2 My Soul (book) 56

Track & Field News Press 45, 144

Truman, Harry S. 18, 71, 105

Trump. Donald 3, 67

TV Channel 33 (Comcast 20 Detroit) 58, 73

TV Channels 2, 4, and 7, Detroit 52, 86

Twain, Mark ix, 40, 47, 105

## U

UAW (United Auto Workers)  51

United States Congress  73

United States Marine Corps  72

United States Senate  66

United States Supreme Court  119

University of Maryland  37

University of Michigan  12, 39

## V

Valentino, Rudolph  78

Villanova University  45

Villa, Pancho  80

## W

Wall Street  66

Washington, George  65, 105

Washington Post  37

Washington Redskins  12

Wayne State University  9, 29, 57, 144

WEXL 1340 AM Detroit  58, 73

What OLD MEN Know (book)  v, 8, 37, 56, 76, 78, 81, 82, 83, 106, 147

Williamsburg, New York  21

WNY Scottish Games  21

Wolverine Human Services  12

Wooten, Willie  viii, 54

World War II  11, 64, 70

## Y

Yeats, W. B.  7

## Z

Zumsteg, Tresa  44, 61

# TWO POSTLUDE POEMS

*Leaves of Ice*

*(in partial tribute to Walt Whitman)*
*Following a freezing rain*
*On a sun-bright winter morn,*
*I was born a bawling bairn*
*In my snow-topped Motown home.*

*Leaves of ice popped up by chance*
*And shone on drooping bits of branch.*
*Sparkling from dark silhouette,*
*They glitter in the winter yet.*

*With somer minor, mixed supports*
*Through the dastard decades since,*
*I've fought folks with frozen hearts*
*And hardened heads and minds of mince.*

*(Some I've loved and some I've not:*
 *The unloved ones I've left to rot.)*

*Today I wish at last to see*
*These sparkly star-tipped branches freed*
*From greedy grip of icy bead*
*And then, in shortened order, sprout*
*New true-grown leaves from free-born seed,*
*Perhaps yet one more time, flat-out.*

*In the Interim:*

*Intimation of Immortality
(in partial tribute to William Wordsworth
and T. S. Eliot)*

*I've raced interim sprinters
In interim races,
Loved interim women In interim places,
Been interim chief of
Detroit's troubled schools
(And of Madison's briefly,
Contending with fools).*

*Between the desire
And the short spasm
Whence once we were sired
To cross the long chasm,
From that fast coming
Until the last going,
Between our first stirring
And final interring,
Indeed, we're all interim*

*Yet just in the interim. . . ??*

# ABOUT THE AUTHOR

**DR. JOHN TELFORD** has been called a "human-rights legend." More frequently—if somewhat less kindly—he has also been called a "lightning rod for controversy."

A conqueror of Olympic champions in the mid-1950s, John Telford retired in 1991 as the Deputy Superintendent of Schools in 98 percent white Rochester, Michigan, where skinheads shot bullets into his home at midnight for aggressively recruiting and hiring minority administrators and for establishing a holiday policy that was fair to non-Christian students. He was fired from two Detroit Public School executive directorships for blowing the whistle on inept and corrupt top officials, and he was fired from a superintendency in a school district in another majority-white suburb for recruiting and enrolling hundreds of Detroit students against the wishes of several hundred white residents. In June 2012, at the unlikely age of 76, the Board of Education appointed him interim Superintendent of the troubled Detroit Public Schools.

He is also an artist, a violinist, an award-winning poet, and the author of The Eye in the Emerald, an as-yet-unpublished 600-page gothic novel set in fifteenth-century Scotland, the historic land of his father's birth.

An amateur boxing champion as a teen, Dr. Telford later was undefeated at 400 meters in Europe as an NCAA All-American sprinter and U.S. Team member. He coached champion high school and college runners and wrote a popular book on the quarter-mile—The Longest Dash. It was published by Track & Field News Press in 1965 and 1971 and sold out in both editions. He was inducted into the Athletic Hall of Fame in 1978 at Wayne State University, where he has held the quarter-mile and 400-meter records now for 56 years. He has written more than a thousand newspaper columns and directed or served on the boards of several human-rights agencies. In the early 1970s, he directed the 3,400-student Division of Basic Education at Macomb County College, where he was suspended for insubordination when he brought in the Black Panthers to speak. More recently, he taught at Wayne State and Oakland Universities.

In 1982, the Kettering Foundation-sponsored Institute for the Development of Educational Activities (IDEA) gave Dr. Telford its Distinguished Educator award. Wayne State named him its Distinguished Alumnus of the Year in 2001, and the Joe Louis Memorial Foundation gave him its Spirit of the Champ Award ten years later-both for his civil-rights writings and activism.

In 2003, the Detroit Finney High School track was named for him.

UPDATE, 2022: At age 86, Dr. John Telford lives alone beside the Detroit River. He has a Detroit radio show on WCHB AM1340 Saturday mornings at 9:30 and Monday evenings at 6:30 and another on WJZZ Internet Television C on Wednesday mornings at 10:00, also streaming on Facebook, YouTube, and Twitter. The author of seven books, he also writes the "Telford Telescope" column in the 'Detroit Native Sun' and can be contacted at DrJohnTelfordEdD@aol.com and (313)460-8272. In 2012, he married Adrienne, the dark-haired principal mentioned on p. 330 of his autobiography, 'A Life on the RUN – Seeking & Safeguarding Social Justice. 'In 2013, he was fired by the Detroit schools' Emergency Financial Manager appointed by Republican governor Rick Snyder when an EM law rescinded by voters was reinstated by a Republican-majority legislature, enabling the EFM to become a fully-powered EM. In 2013 he ran unsuccessfully for Mayor of Detroit and for the Detroit school board in 2014. A newly-elected Detroit school board named him its Poet-in-Residence in 2017.

On Jan 7, 2021, he lost Adrienne (pictured with him on the back cover) to cancer and memorialized her thus:

*She dreams in raptured revery*
*Of waterfalls and revelry—*
*Of scenes unseen and multi-hued*
*By bubbling brooklets never viewed.*
*She roams rain forests new and green*
*And drifts down rivers blue and clean.*
*She sees a white-capped tide arising*
*Beneath a far and wide horizon.*
*She sails celestial starlit seas*
*In universal galaxies.*

# ORDER FORM

*Creative Insubordination: 40 Successful Strategies*
**by Dr. John Telford**

Dr. Wayne Dyer, who penned the Introduction to Telford's timelessly philosophical book What OLD MEN Know, says of Creative Insubordination: "John's laser-like Strategies and superbly sardonic humor foil arrogant autocrats, and his poems are explosive." Detroit School Board Lamar Lemmons says, "John Telford's message and some of his methods recall magnificent echoes of the righteous revolutionaries of old. He is a natural force unfettered by convention and defiant of bungling bureaucracies." Says prominent trial lawyer Fred Lauck: "From his wild bravado on Detroit's hardscrabble streets to his lifelong battles with corporate bureaucrats, John Telford now eloquently gives us his Creatively Insubordinate strategies to confound inflexible oligarchs and oligarchies."

You'll want to read this spellbinding book nonstop from cover to cover.

ISBN: 978-1-958030-72-1 / Softcover / 168 pages / 2023 / $10.99 USA
ISBN: 978-1-958030-89-9 / Hardcover / 168 pages / 2023 / $25.99 USA
ISBN: 978-1-958030-73-8 / eBook / 2023 / $3.99 USA

No. of Copies    _____


Name            _____
Address         _____
City/State/Zip  _____
Daytime Phone   _____

Please add 6% sales tax for books shipped to a Michigan address.

www.ingramcontent.com/pod-product-compliance
Lightning Source LLC
LaVergne TN
LVHW011942070526
838202LV00054B/4763